Dutch Painting

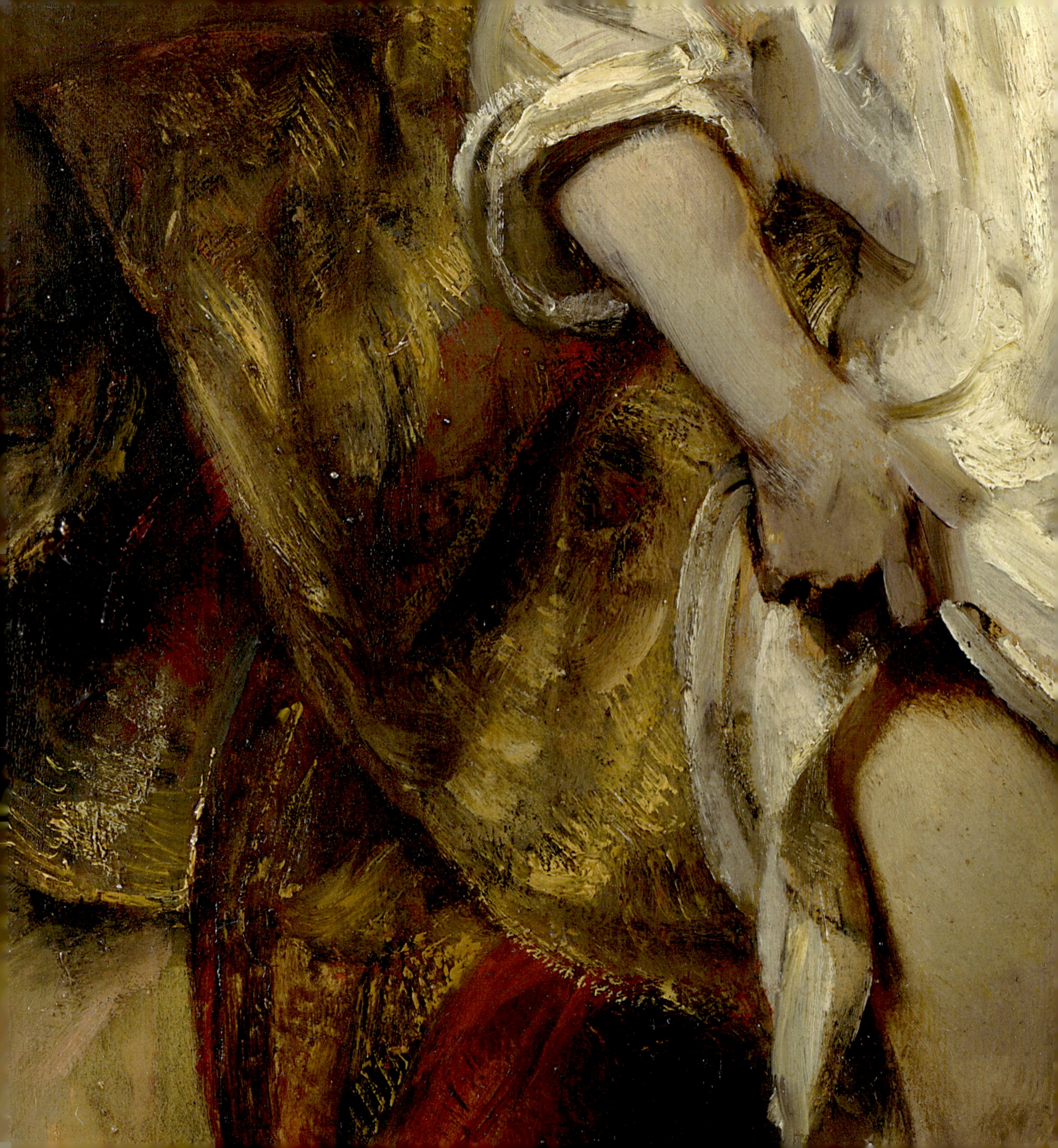

Dutch Painting

National Gallery Company, London
Distributed by Yale University Press

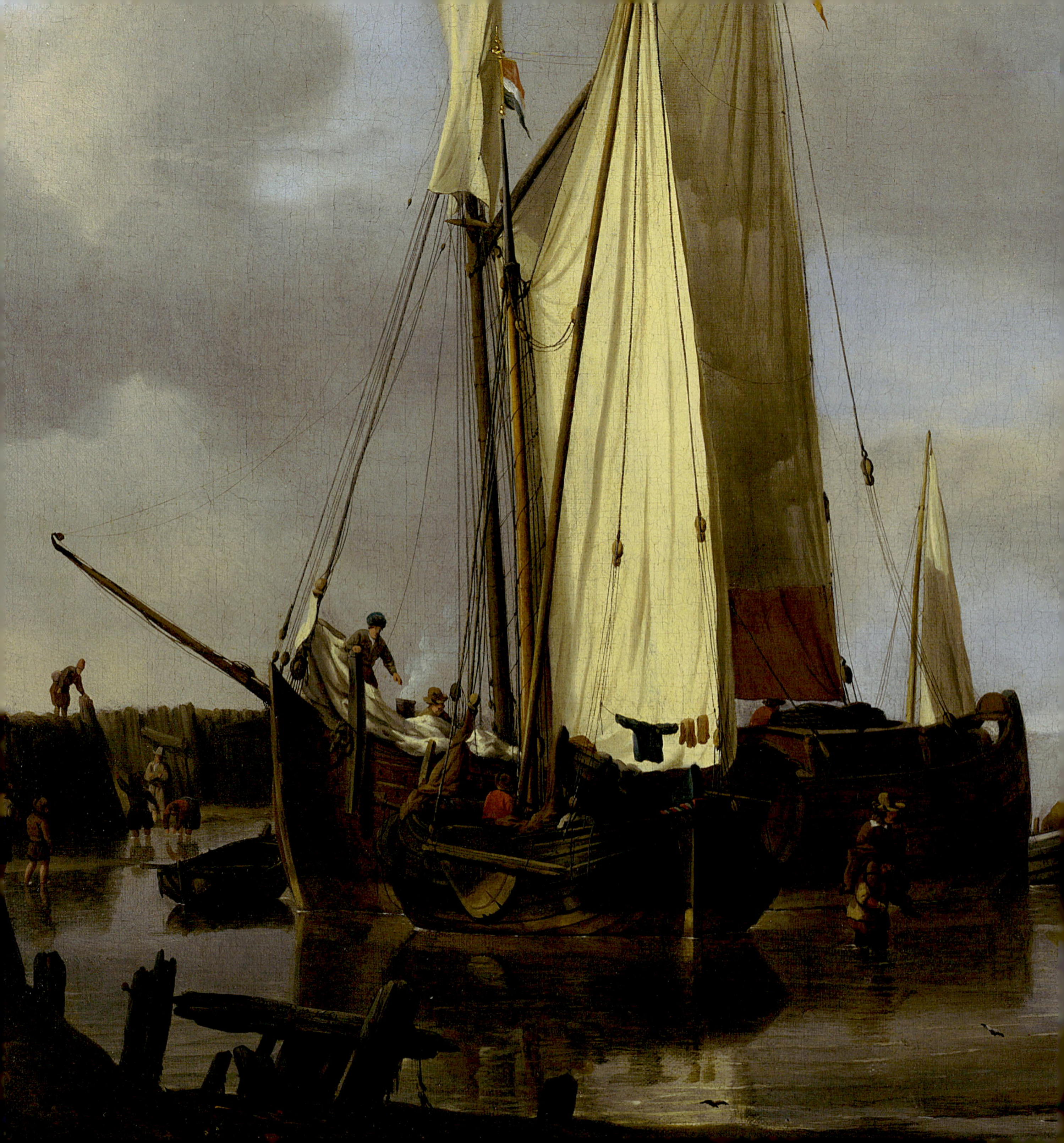

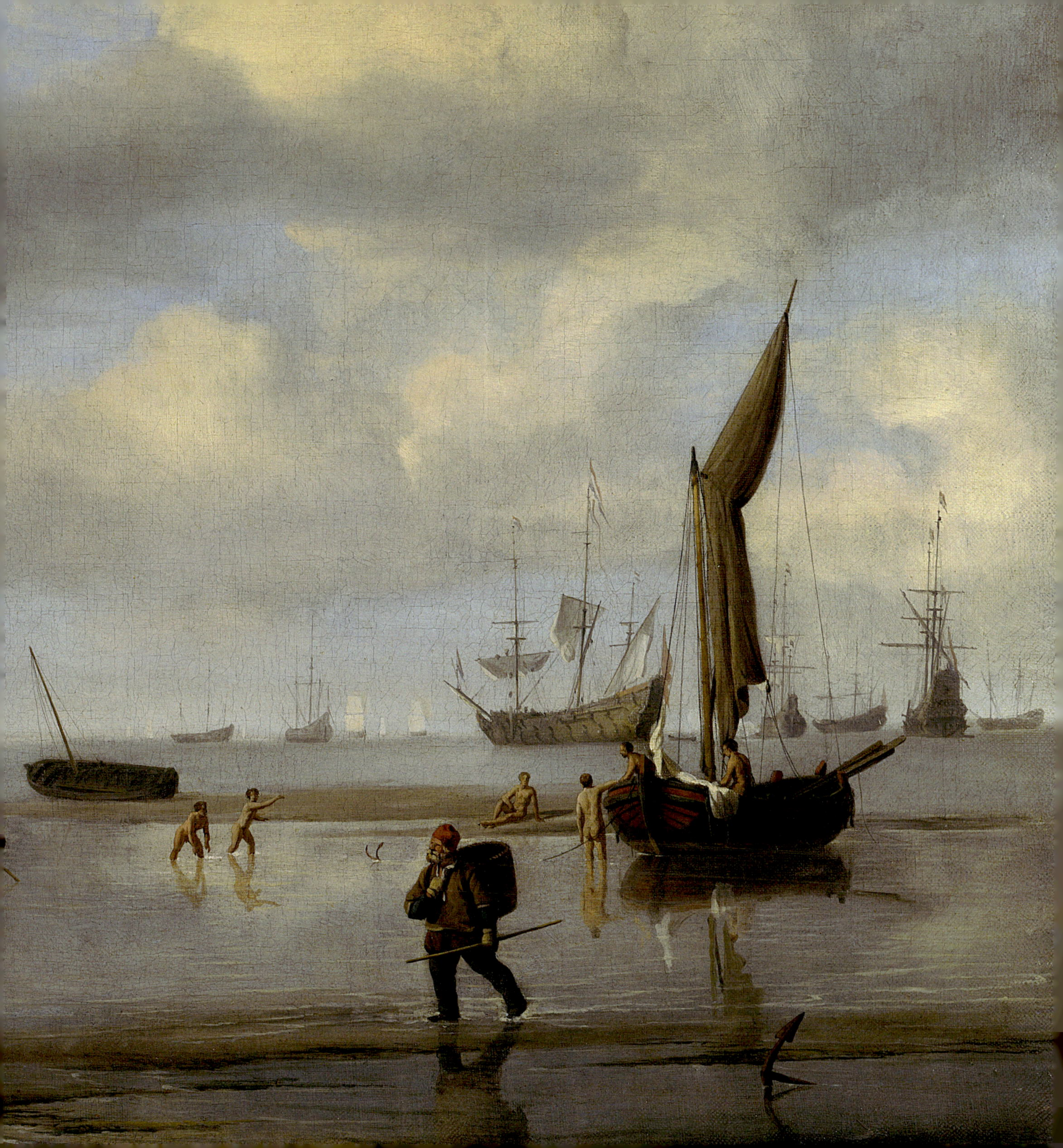

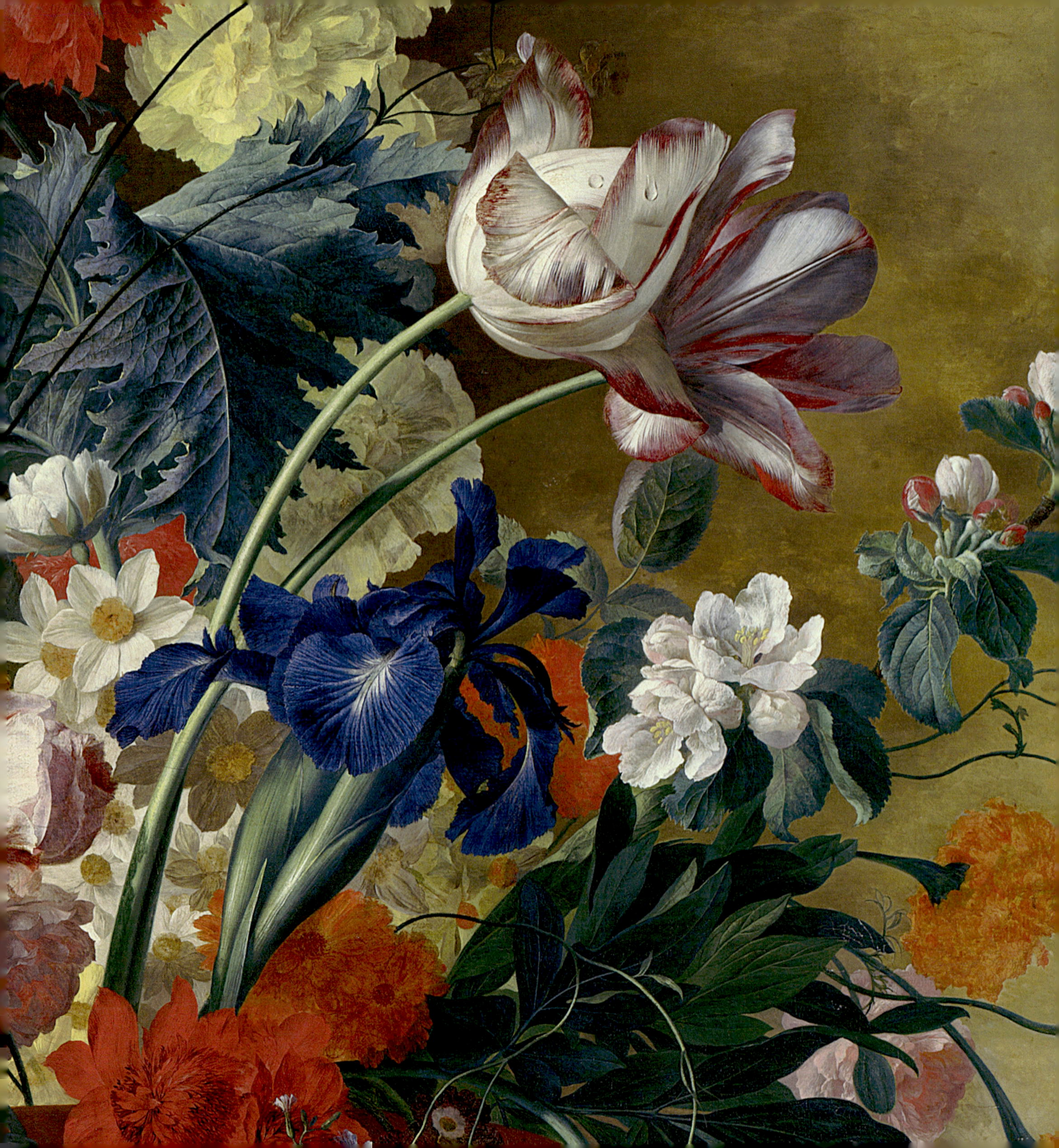

Dutch painting in the seventeenth century

Marjorie E. Wieseman

Dutch paintings of the seventeenth century are a favourite of many museum goers, in part because of the comfortable sense of familiarity derived from their deceptively realistic depiction of the everyday world. Unlike the art of earlier ages, or indeed that of most European countries in the seventeenth century, Dutch paintings seem to open a window directly onto the past: landscapes and seascapes, portraits, still lifes and scenes of everyday life – it would seem that nothing was too humble or mundane to merit the attention of a Dutch painter's brush, and all of it recorded with scrupulous fidelity. There were unquestionably great geniuses among seventeenth-century Dutch painters – Rembrandt, Frans Hals, Johannes Vermeer – but the real strength and miracle of this 'golden age' lies in the sheer abundance of paintings of extraordinarily high quality, produced by talented artists working not just in major urban centres like Amsterdam or Utrecht, but also in smaller cities like Haarlem, Leiden, Delft and Dordrecht; and more distant towns like Zwolle, Deventer and Middelburg.

A number of factors – religious, political, intellectual, social and economic – facilitated this extraordinary flowering. For much of the sixteenth century, the Netherlands was governed by Catholic Spain, but in the aftermath of the Protestant rebellion that began in 1566, the northern provinces (eventually known as the United Provinces, and today as the Netherlands) began a protracted struggle for independence that was concluded only in 1648 (pp. 34–5). (The southern provinces remained under Spanish control, eventually coalescing into modern-day Belgium.) Unlike most European countries, with power concentrated in the hands of royalty or the Catholic church, the largely Protestant Dutch Republic was governed by an appointed stadholder, or governor, in conjunction with representatives from the various provinces (the States General). The most powerful and influential forces in the land were not courtiers and aristocrats, but enormously wealthy merchants, industrialists and city officials. And the seventeenth-century Dutch Republic *was* wealthy, thanks in part to an extensive international network of maritime trade, vigorous industrial enterprise and the assiduous cultivation of livestock and agriculture. Moreover, the religious and political freedoms offered by the young republic lured ambitious immigrants from across Europe: skilled

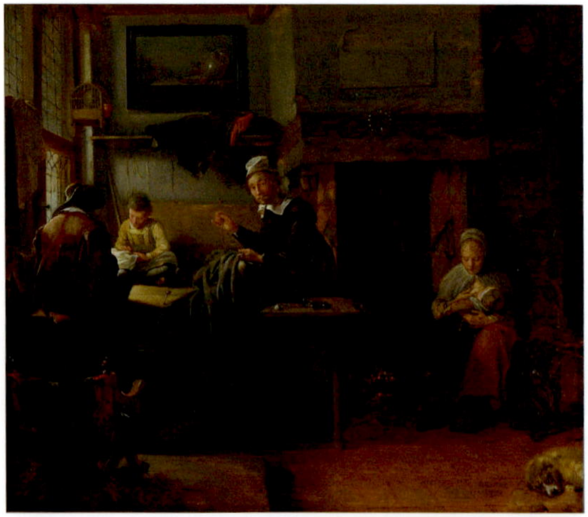

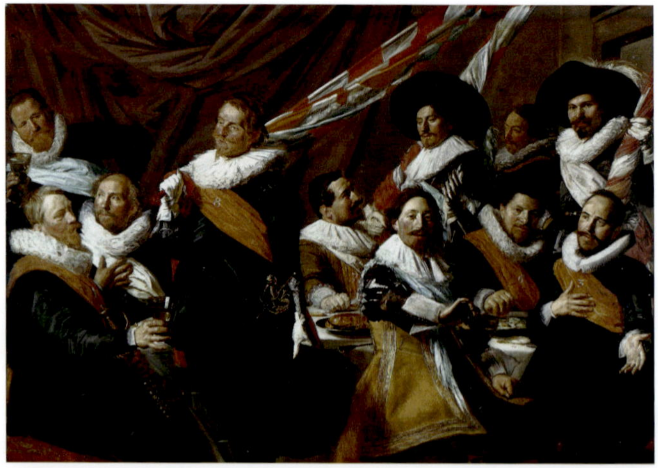

Fig. 1
Quiringh van Brekelenkam, *Interior of a Tailor's Shop*, about 1655–61
Oil on oak, 42.7 x 50 cm
National Gallery, London

Fig. 2
Frans Hals, *Banquet of the Officers of the St George Civic Guard*, 1627
Oil on canvas, 179 x 257.5 cm
Frans Hals Museum, Haarlem

craftsmen, merchants, industrialists and intellectuals brought their creativity, resources and contacts to this small land, spurring the Dutch economy to unprecedented growth.

Understandably, these prosperous Dutchmen and -women looked for ways to display their newfound wealth, and it seems that decorating their private homes with paintings and comfortable furnishings was a popular way of doing so (pp. 46–7). Indeed, foreign visitors to the Netherlands were astonished to find paintings wherever they looked: an English traveller in 1640 noted that even 'butchers and bakers ... blacksmiths, cobblers etc.' adorned their homes with paintings (fig. 1). At about the same time (1641), the English writer John Evelyn was surprised not only by the abundance of pictures he saw for sale at a fair in Rotterdam, but also by the money 'a common farmer' was willing to invest in them.

The seventeenth-century Dutch Republic provided a uniquely encouraging situation for an enterprising artist: with virtually no commissions forth-coming from the Catholic church or a powerful court, a painter was no longer dependent upon those bodies for his or her livelihood and was therefore less restricted in choosing what to paint. To be sure, there were still competitive commissions to decorate public buildings, or to portray the leaders of civic militia companies or the governing bodies of professional guilds and charitable organisations (fig. 2); indeed, many of these group portraits contributed substantially to the innovative character of seventeenth-century

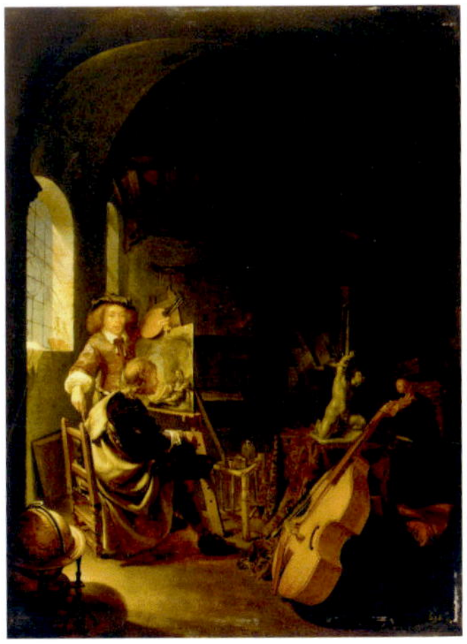

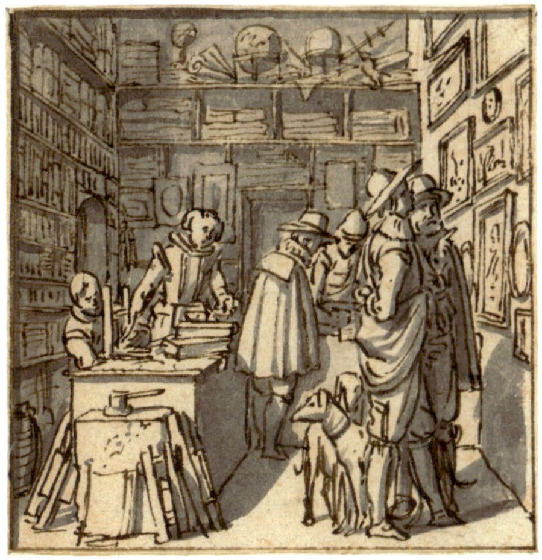

Fig. 3
Frans van Mieris, *Self Portrait of the Painter in his Studio*, about 1659
Oil on oak, 63.9 x 46.8 cm
Gemäldegalerie Alte Meister, Dresden

Fig. 4
Dirk or Salomon de Bray, *Men and Two Dogs in a Bookseller's Shop*, about 1628
Pen and brown ink with grey wash, 76 x 76 mm
Rijksmuseum, Amsterdam

Dutch painting. But most painters worked for the broad middle class: from wealthy merchants and city officials to butchers and tailors, there was a painter and a painting available to suit just about every taste and pocketbook.

From the late sixteenth century artists developed a range of new genres and subject matter in paintings that responded to their bourgeois clientele's desire for pictures that were largely celebrations of the world around them. Images of the native Dutch landscape (pp. 57, 81, 91) or its tidy cities (pp. 43, 89, 93), views of calm waterways and open seas (pp. 64–5, 71, 83), still lifes displaying everyday implements and exotic treasures (pp. 19, 31, 95) and scenes depicting the mundane activities of virtually every segment of Dutch society (pp. 17, 49, 79), were among the most inventive, and highly sought after, categories of painting over the course of the century. While an artist might paint a picture at the specific request of a patron – as would certainly be the case in with a portrait – probably the majority of pictures made in the Dutch Republic in the seventeenth century were produced for the open market, and sold either at the artist's studio (fig. 3), in shops (fig. 4) or at the sort of fairs visited by Evelyn.

Painting for the open market gave an artist the freedom to paint according to his abilities and interests, giving rise to one of the most distinctive characteristics of Dutch painting, that of specialisation. Although there were always artists who turned their hand to a wide range of subject matter – Rembrandt, for example, painted biblical, mythological and allegorical subjects, portraits and character studies, even landscapes and still lifes (pp. 37, 39, 53, 55), and was a celebrated printmaker as well – most focused their energies on just one or two subjects. With so many painters competing against each other to sell their pictures in an open market, it was to each painter's benefit to identify a 'niche' and distinguish himself within it, constantly refining and improving his or her product to bring it to the highest possible level. For example, Hendrick Avercamp made the most of the Netherlands' frigid winters and abundant waterways to become the first artist to specialise in lively (and enduringly popular) scenes of people enjoying themselves on the ice (p. 17). Inspired by the gardens of his native city of Middelburg and a scholarly community of botanists and horticulturalists, Ambrosius Bosschaert the Elder crafted exquisite, precisely detailed and vividly coloured flower pieces that beguiled collectors and attracted many imitators (p. 19). Later in the century, Jacob van Ruisdael painted almost exclusively landscapes, but invested each view of forests, dunes, grainfields, waterfalls or coastlines with characteristic drama and towering cloud-filled skies (pp. 81, 83).

Specialisation often meant focusing on a specific type of subject matter, but it could also take the form of developing a distinctive painterly style, or approach to subject matter. Inspired by the example of the Italian painter Caravaggio, painters like Gerrit van Honthorst and Hendrick ter Brugghen became famous for their depiction of earthy characters and their use of dramatic lighting effects (pp. 23, 27). Frans Hals developed a highly personal, loose style of painting that gave liveliness and spontaneity to his portraits and figure studies (p. 25). Almost diametrically opposed to Hals's dazzling brushwork was the fine detail and smooth, enamel-like finish of paintings by Gerrit Dou (p. 79), whose work commanded enormous prices and inspired generations of followers, the so-called Leiden 'fine painters' (*fijnschilders*). A skillful orchestration of lighting effects and a varied and thickly textured application of paint, a penetrating study of character and emotion and an often unusual choice of subject matter, became hallmarks of works by Rembrandt and his followers. On the other hand, Jan Steen produced a wide variety of genre scenes, historical subjects and portraits, but all are informed by his lively wit and familiarity with popular literature (pp. 67, 69). In his own day, Johannes Vermeer (pp. 85, 87) was respected as a painter of 'perspectives' – paintings of interiors that emphasise the illusion of three-dimensional space – but today we recognise his true speciality to be the creation of an almost trance-like calm that gives his paintings their mysterious allure.

Dutch painters had plenty to inspire them within the borders of their own country, but they were not ignorant of developments in other countries, or averse to incorporating them into their own work. The acid colours, strange, sinuous figures and claustrophobic excess of Joachim Wtewael's *Judgement of Paris* (p. 21) reflects the influence of Mannerist art as practised at the court of the Holy Roman Emperor, Rudolf II, in Prague. Within just a few years, however, Wtewael's younger Utrecht colleagues Honthorst and Ter Brugghen had turned their attention to Italy and were incorporating the dramatic impact of Caravaggio's realism into their work. Indeed, Italy was a steady source of inspiration for artists throughout the seventeenth century, although that inspiration manifested itself in a variety of ways. While figure painters looked to antique sculptures and paintings by Renaissance and 'modern' (seventeenth-century) masters, landscape painters were most profoundly drawn to the golden Mediterranean light (p. 59). In fact, the warm glow of the southern sun, and its effects upon the landscape, were so admired that even artists who had never been to Italy – notably Aelbert Cuyp – specialised in incorporating it into their works (pp. 60–1).

The artistic interaction between the Dutch Republic and other European countries in the seventeenth century was not limited to Dutch artists reaping inspiration from their travels abroad, however. The quality, diversity and unique character of Dutch paintings was quickly recognised by collectors and connoisseurs across Europe. A handful of Dutch artists found work at foreign courts (Samuel van Hoogstraten and Willem van de Velde, pp. 45–7, 71, both worked in England, for example), but more often their work found wider circulation through foreign agents and collectors who made visits to artists' studios a regular part of their travels through the Netherlands (fig. 3). It is in part because of the interest and efforts of those devoted travellers that seventeenth-century Dutch paintings can be found in so many collections around the world, and have become so familiar to us today.

Over the years, the National Gallery has come to house one of the finest collections of Dutch painting outside the Netherlands. When the Gallery began in 1824, there were just three Dutch paintings in the collection – curious, given that Dutch paintings had been enormously popular with collectors in Britain for several generations. In its early years, the Gallery was focused on acquiring Italian pictures, especially 'large pictures of eminence'; intimately scaled Dutch pictures, no matter how exquisitely wrought, were thought more suitable for decorating domestic spaces than for display in the grand rooms of a public art gallery. Still, major works were added to the collection at regular intervals: Rembrandt's *Woman bathing in a Stream* (p. 53), for example, came to the Gallery in 1830 through a bequest from the Reverend William Holwell Carr (1758–1830). When Charles Lock Eastlake (1793–1865), Keeper and Director of the National Gallery, saw the same artist's *Self Portrait at the Age of 34* (p. 39) at a Paris exhibition in 1861, he immediately identified it as a desirable acquisition for the Gallery and quickly negotiated its purchase. Perhaps the single most important acquisition of Dutch pictures was the purchase of the Peel collection in 1871, for £75,000. Sir Robert Peel (1788–1850), who served twice as Prime Minister, had assembled a spectacular group of seventeenth-century Dutch paintings, often paying premium prices to secure the pictures he wanted. The 55 Dutch paintings from the Peel collection included Ostade's *Alchemist*, Dou's *Poulterer's Shop*, Hobbema's *The Avenue at Middelharnis*, De Hooch's *The Courtyard of a House in Delft*, and Van de Velde the Younger's *Dutch Vessels close Inshore at Low Tide, and Men Bathing* (pp. 77, 79, 91, 49 and 71). Another important group of Dutch paintings entered the Gallery in 1876, with the generous bequest of the industrialist MP, Wynn Ellis (1790–1875). The Ellis collection was particularly strong in landscapes and seascapes, including Italianate works like Jan Both's poetic *A Rocky Italian Landscape with Herdsmen and Muleteers* (p. 59), and six paintings by Jacob van Ruisdael, among which was the sublime *Landscape with a Ruined Castle and a Church* (p. 81).

As the Gallery's holdings of Dutch pictures grew in size and scope, deliberate steps were taken to shape the collection, in part by seeking out key works by major artists – among them, Johannes Vermeer. Although Vermeer is today one of the world's most beloved artists, he was virtually unknown before his 'rediscovery' by critics in the 1860s. The pursuit of a Vermeer for the collection began almost immediately, but it was a while before the search met with success. Indeed, Gallery Director Charles Locke Eastlake (1836–1906) rejected several paintings before the *Young Woman standing at a Virginal* (p. 85) was finally acquired in 1892. The Gallery's second Vermeer, *Young Woman seated at a Virginal* (p. 87), entered the collection in 1910 with the bequest of George Salting (1835–1909); this bequest also included paintings by Saenredam (p. 29), Paulus Potter (p. 57), and Jan Steen (p. 67), among other seventeenth-century Dutch masters.

In the twentieth and twenty-first centuries, Dutch paintings have entered the

National Gallery collection at a more stately pace. Many of the works acquired already had a long and distinguished history in British collections, attesting to the longevity of the British taste for Dutch art. Gerrit van Honthorst's magisterial *Christ before the High Priest* (p. 23), for example, was in a London collection by 1840; another important Caravaggesque work, *The Concert* by Hendrick ter Brugghen (p. 27), was in England as early as 1700; and Aelbert Cuyp's luminous *River Landscape with Horseman and Peasants* (pp. 60–1) had entered a prestigious English collection in 1760. The most recent addition to the collection, Ambrosius Bosschaert the Elder's exquisite *Still Life of Flowers in a Wan-Li Vase* (p. 19), is ample proof of the Gallery's continuing commitment to acquiring works of the highest calibre for the enjoyment of the museum-going public.

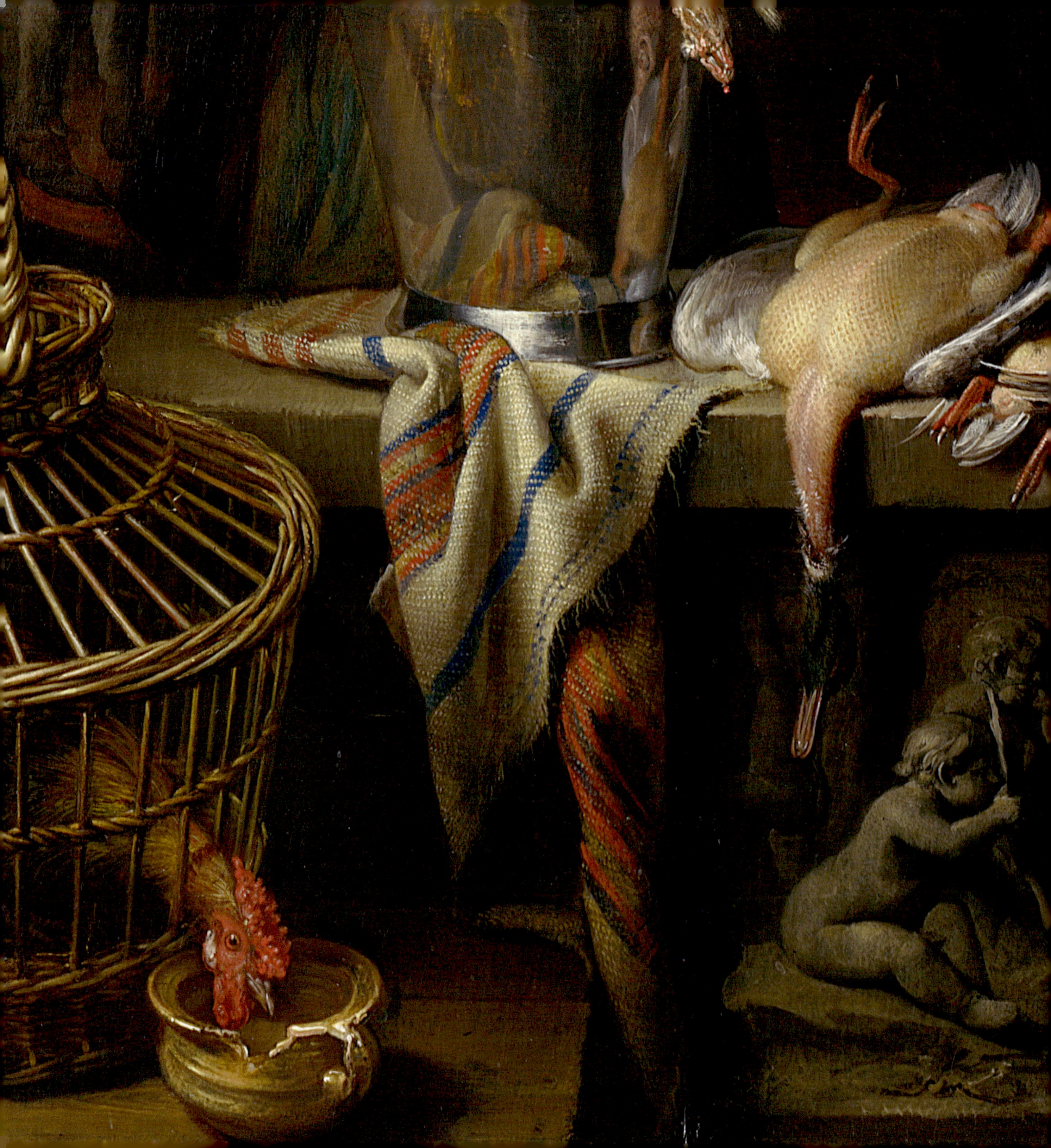

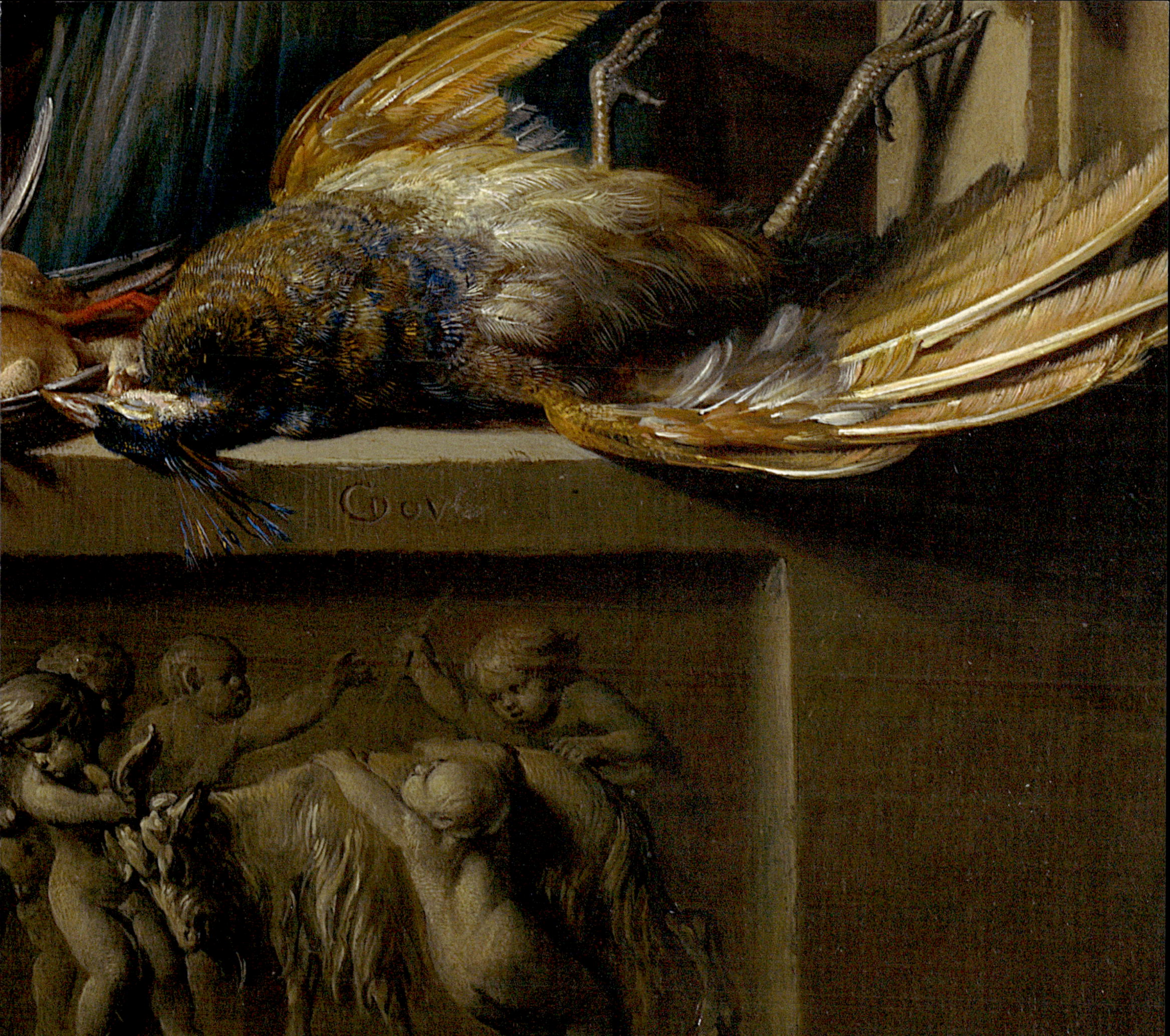

Hendrick Avercamp

(1585–1634)

A Winter Scene with Skaters near a Castle, about 1608–9

Oil on oak, 40.7 x 40.7 cm

The very first depictions of winter scenes were backdrops to the seasonal 'labours' in illuminated manuscripts. Avercamp was key to the development of winter scenes as a specialist genre in Dutch painting – inspired by the work of the sixteenth-century Flemish painter Pieter Bruegel the Elder, the first artist to paint an independent winter landscape. During the seventeenth century north-west Europe was beset by a series of unusually severe winters, and Avercamp found ample inspiration for his clever depictions of people at work and play in the ice and snow.

Avercamp's early winter scenes often employ a high viewpoint, which enabled him to fill the landscape with a variety of lively details. The skeletal tree in the foreground, another device Avercamp used often, frames the scene and draws the eye into the middle ground. This motif, along with the imagined castle and citizens at play, can be found in contemporary prints that must have influenced Avercamp's painting. In his later work the artist abandoned these traditional compositional techniques, but retained his subtle palette of earth tones, pinks and greys.

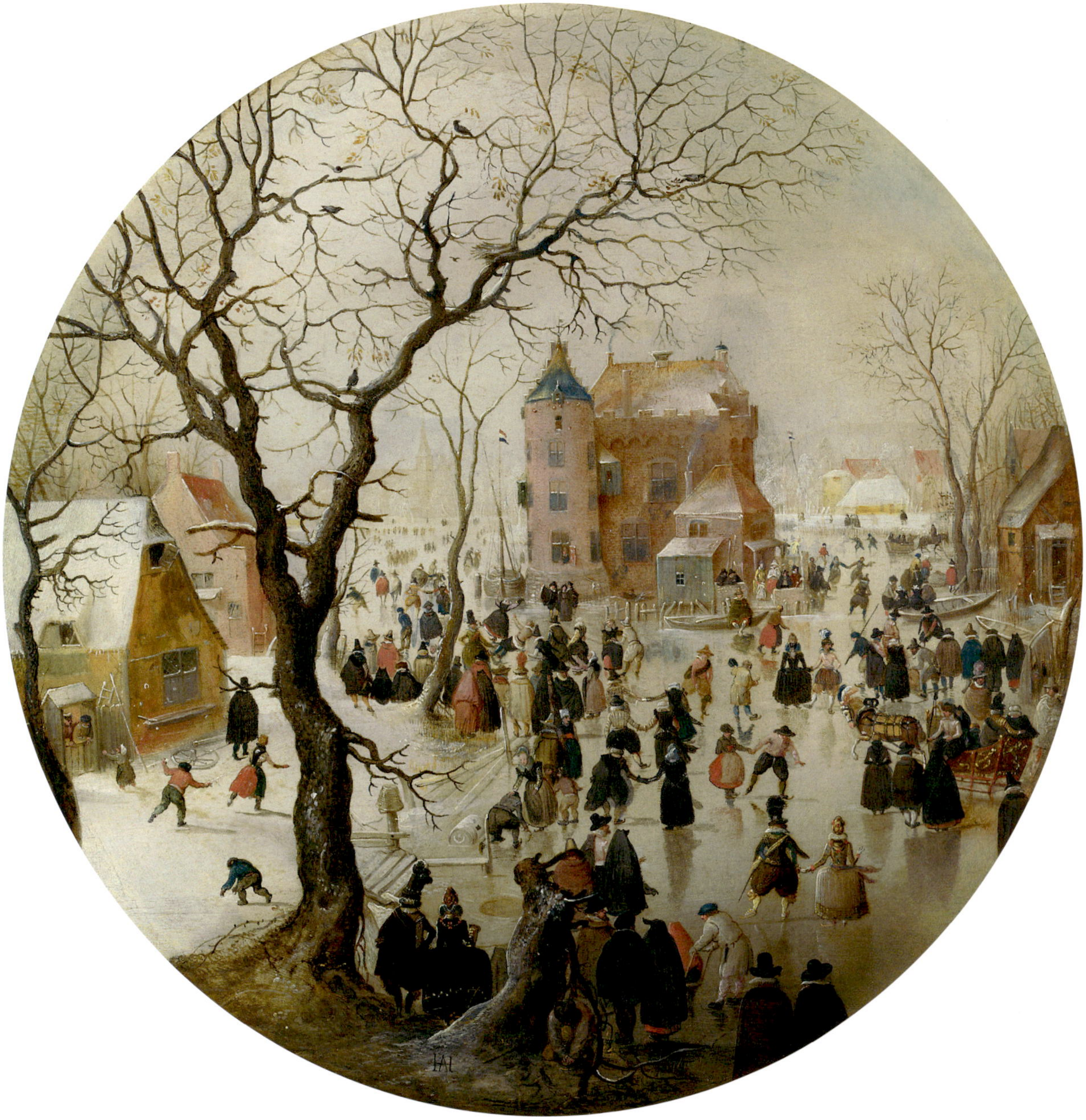

Ambrosius Bosschaert the Elder

(1573–1621)

A Still Life of Flowers in a Wan-Li Vase, 1609–10

Oil on copper panel,
68.6 x 50.7 cm
Accepted by HM Government in lieu of Inheritance Tax and allocated to the National Gallery, 2010

One of the first Dutch artists to specialise in flower painting, Bosschaert drew inspiration from Middelburg's botanical gardens and the exotic treasures imported by the Dutch East India Company. In his compositions, rare blossoms are held in exquisite vases, often flanked by costly seashells culled from foreign oceans. Many are painted on smooth copper panels, enhancing the extraordinary detail and precision of his brushwork.

Bosschaert did not restrict himself to depicting only flowers that were in bloom at the same time, but instead gathered the most beautiful examples from all seasons. He often repeated individual specimens in several different compositions, suggesting that he relied on a stock of drawn or painted studies.

This painting features an array of spring and summer flowers, mostly exotic cultivars rather than native species: several varieties of roses and tulips, as well as columbine, anemone, fritillaria, iris, carnation, marigold, daffodil, lily-of-the-valley, hyacinth and rosemary. A butterfly and numerous insects ply random leaves and petals. The Chinese blue-and-white porcelain vase was a prized collector's item, imported to Europe by Dutch and Portuguese trading vessels and there fitted with a gilt mount.

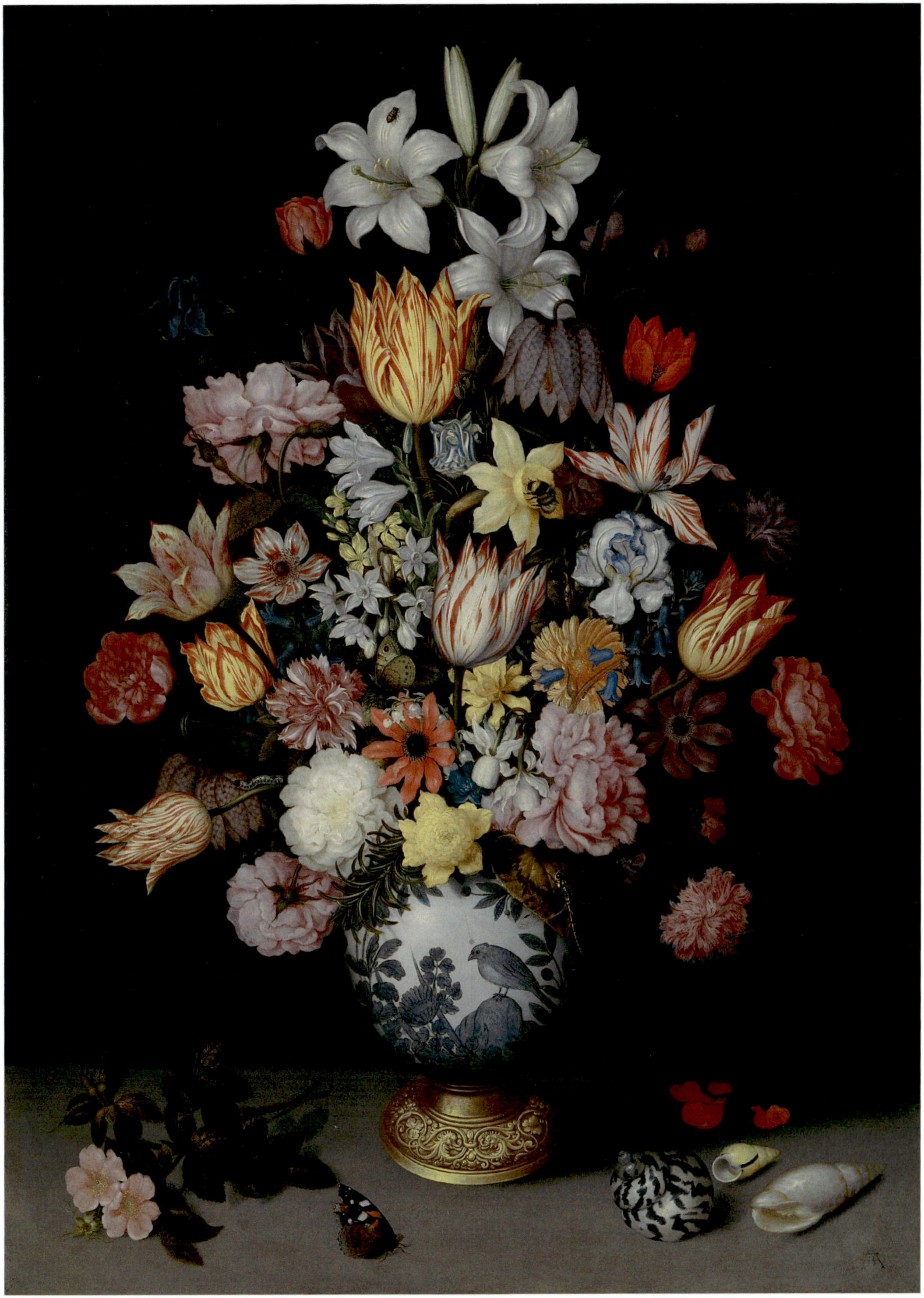

Joachim Wtewael

(1566–1638)

The Judgement of Paris, 1615

Oil on oak, 59.8 x 79.2 cm
Bequeathed by Claude Dickason Rotch, 1962

According to Ovid's *Metamorphoses*, all the gods of Olympus were invited to celebrate the wedding of Peleus and Thetis – except Eris, god of discord. In revenge, Eris threw a golden apple inscribed 'For the fairest' onto the banquet table, prompting a quarrel between Juno, goddess of wealth, Minerva, goddess of wisdom and victory, and Venus, goddess of beauty. The Trojan prince Paris was called upon to settle the dispute. Each goddess offered him a bribe, but Venus won the contest by promising Paris the hand of Helen of Troy, an offer that triggered a series of disastrous events culminating in the Trojan War. Wtewael's densely packed image gives no inkling of the horrors to come. Venus receives the golden apple from Paris; Juno and Minerva stand to the left and right respectively. The gods of Olympus are gathered in the background.

Wtewael was one of the leading exponents of Mannerism in the Netherlands. Characteristic of his later style are the exaggerated elegance and artifice of the elongated figures, coupled with a lavish display of highly naturalistic flora and fauna. Although the story of Paris's Judgement warns of the consequences of yielding to the sensual temptations of love, the pervasive sensuality of Wtewael's depiction is specifically intended to beguile the viewer.

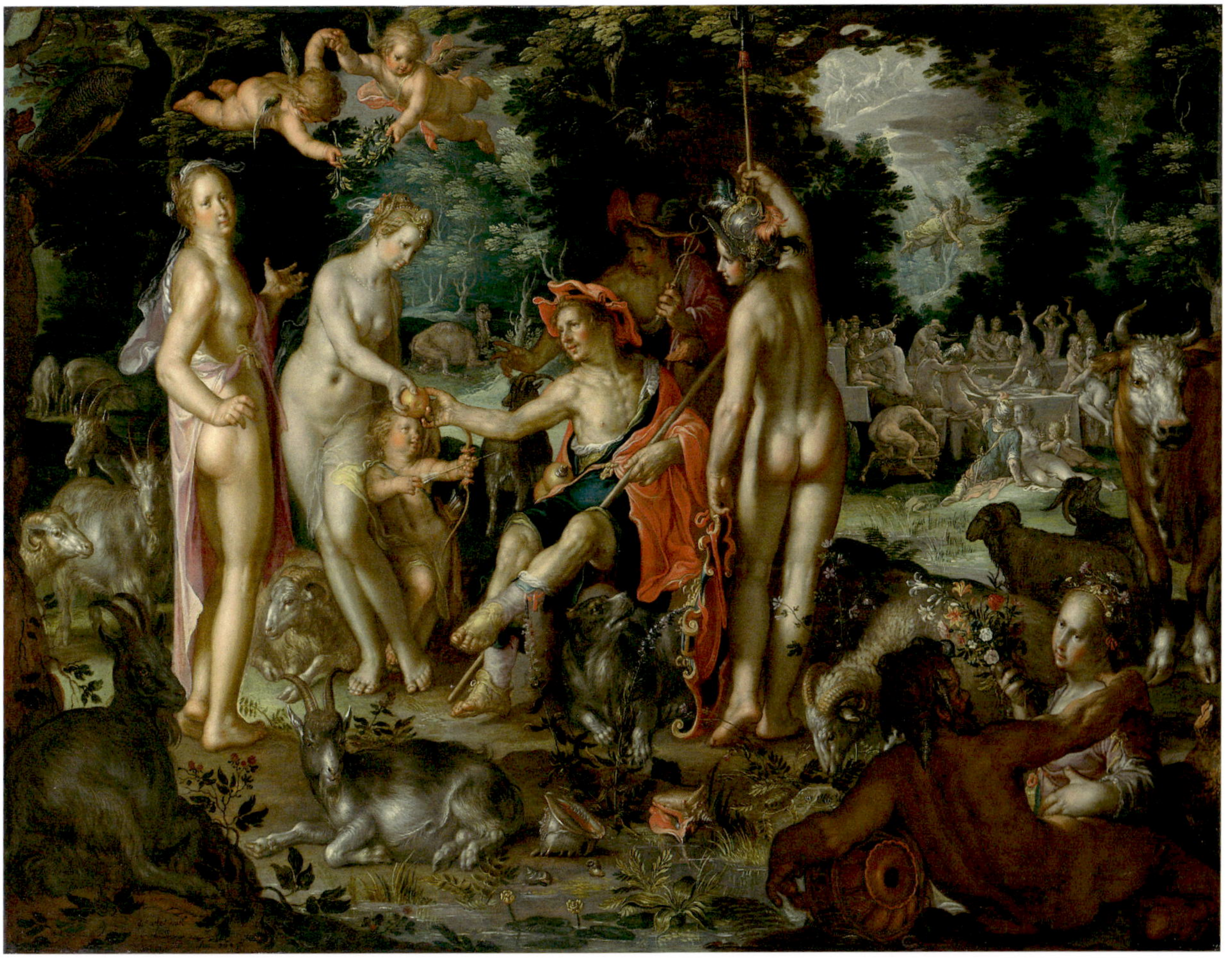

Gerrit van Honthorst

(1592–1656)

Christ before the High Priest, about 1617

Oil on canvas, 272 x 183 cm

As a young man Honthorst journeyed to Rome – encouraged, perhaps, by his Catholic faith as much as the desire to further his artistic education. He made this monumental work, the masterpiece of his Roman years, for the Marchese Vincenzo Giustiniani, his principal patron in the city. With hands bound before him, Christ has been brought before the high priest (possibly Caiaphas?) to be questioned about his teachings. The cavernous chamber is lit by the flame of a single candle, which sharply models nearby objects and casts distant ones into a shadowy half-light. The subtle manipulation of lighting effects and the naturalism and stark simplicity of the composition, which strips the narrative to its bare essentials, reveal Honthorst's debt to the Italian master Caravaggio (1571–1610).

Buoyed by his Italian success, Honthorst returned to Utrecht in 1620. He became the most famous of the Dutch followers of Caravaggio, the 'Utrecht Caravaggisti'.

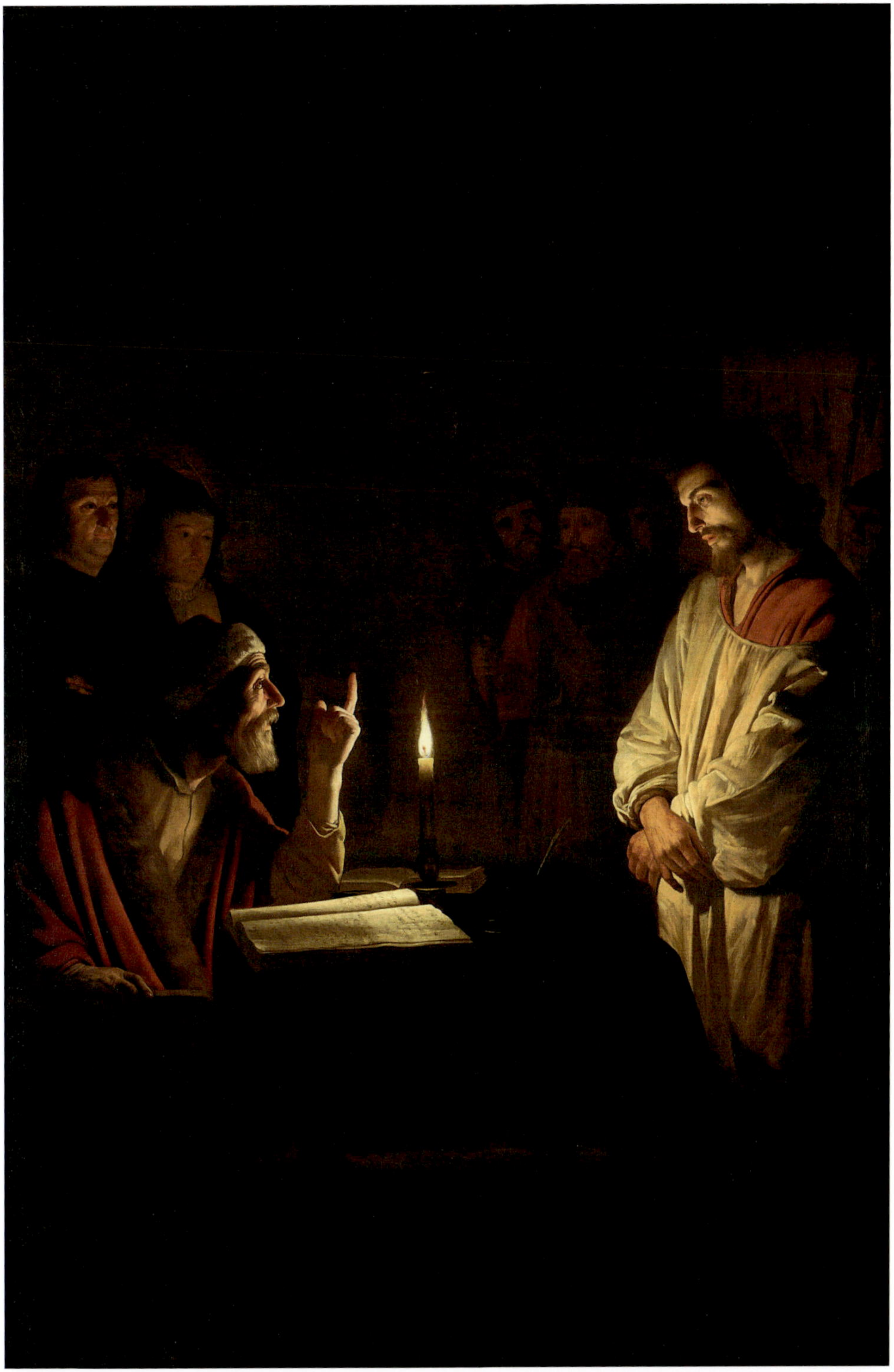

Frans Hals

(about 1582/3–1666)

Young Man holding a Skull (Vanitas), 1626–8

Oil on canvas, 92.2 x 80.8 cm

Bold and confident, this ruddy-cheeked boy holds a skull in one hand and gestures so forcefully with the other that his fingertips seem to burst through the canvas. His shoulders are swathed in a bulky cloth; his tousled hair topped by a soft hat adorned with an improbably long feather. No other elements compete for our attention: just the presence of the figure and the brilliance of the technique. The loose, slashing and economical brushstrokes with which Hals rendered light and form are unprecedented and unequalled in the seventeenth century.

The skull suggests that the painting was intended as a *vanitas*, an expression of the transience of life and the inevitability of death. The spontaneity of the brushwork and Hals's ability to express a momentary likeness are an inspired complement to a meditation on the fleeting nature of time.

For almost two centuries after the artist's death, prevailing taste favoured smooth, highly finished paintings, and the freedom of Hals's brushwork was disparaged as sloppy, negligent and indicative of a debauched lifestyle. By 1900, however, the advent of Impressionism and a concern for naturalistic observation encouraged renewed admiration for Hals's virtuoso brushwork.

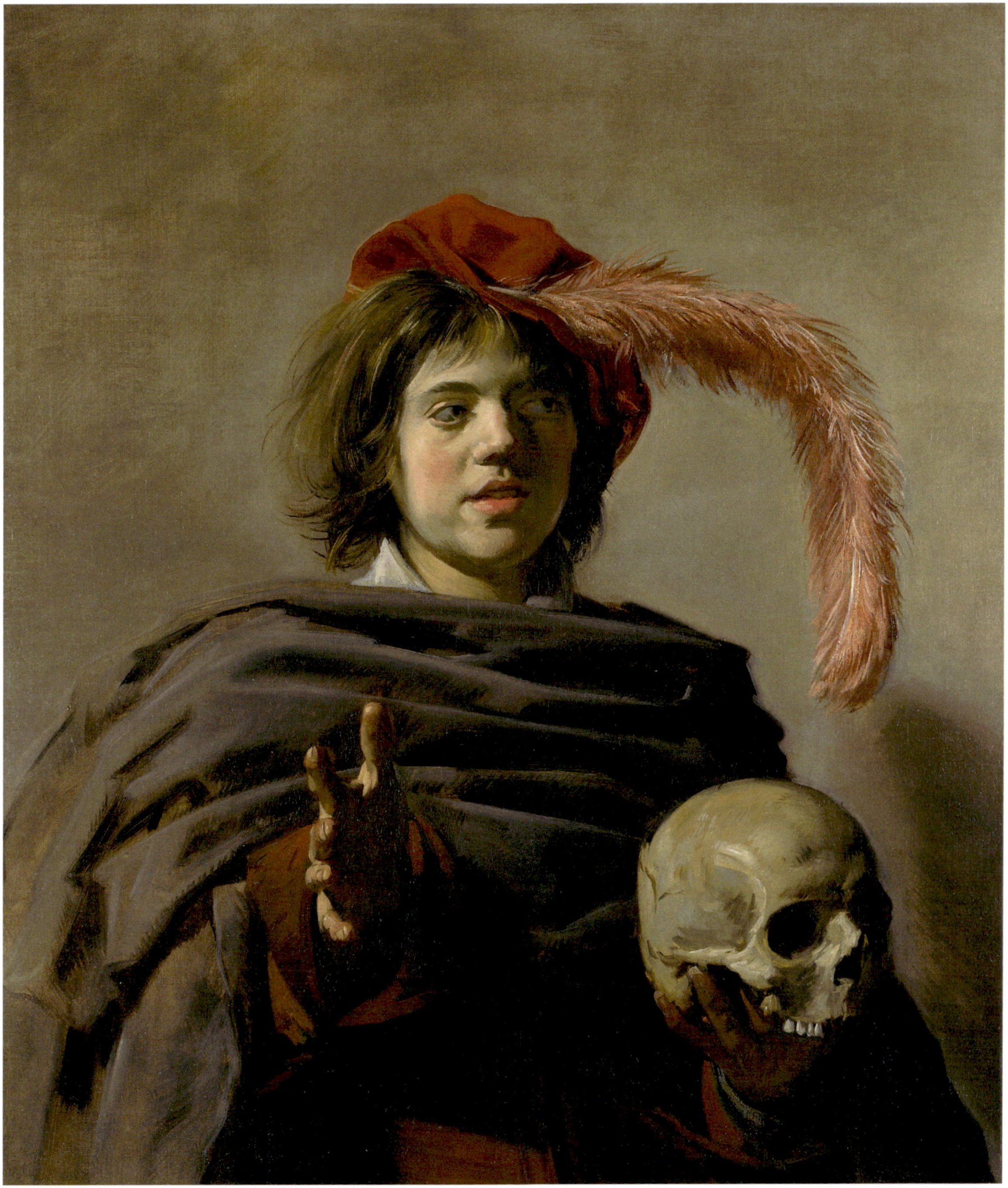

Hendrick ter Brugghen

(1588–1629)

The Concert, about 1626

Oil on canvas, 99.1 x 116.8 cm
Bought with contributions from the National Heritage Memorial Fund, The Art Fund and The Pilgrim Trust, 1983

Ter Brugghen, like Honthorst (p. 22), was a Utrecht painter who made the pilgrimage to Rome. Upon his return north in 1615 he adopted a modern approach to traditional Netherlandish subjects, both sacred and secular, that incorporated the latest Italian innovations: a radical naturalism and dramatic chiaroscuro inspired by the paintings of Caravaggio.

These earthy musicians are not drawing-room dilettantes; their flamboyant garments are a picturesque interpretation of the colourful costumes worn by itinerant performers. The grapes and wineglass in the foreground are a reference to Bacchus, the god of wine and revelry. Ter Brugghen brings intimacy and immediacy to his subject by cropping the scene tightly around the figures, using candlelight to create a mood. Where Honthorst aimed for dramatic tension, Ter Brugghen coaxes an elegiac reverie from the candle's flame. The use of a double light source – the candle in the foreground and the oil lamp hanging on the rear wall – is particularly sophisticated.

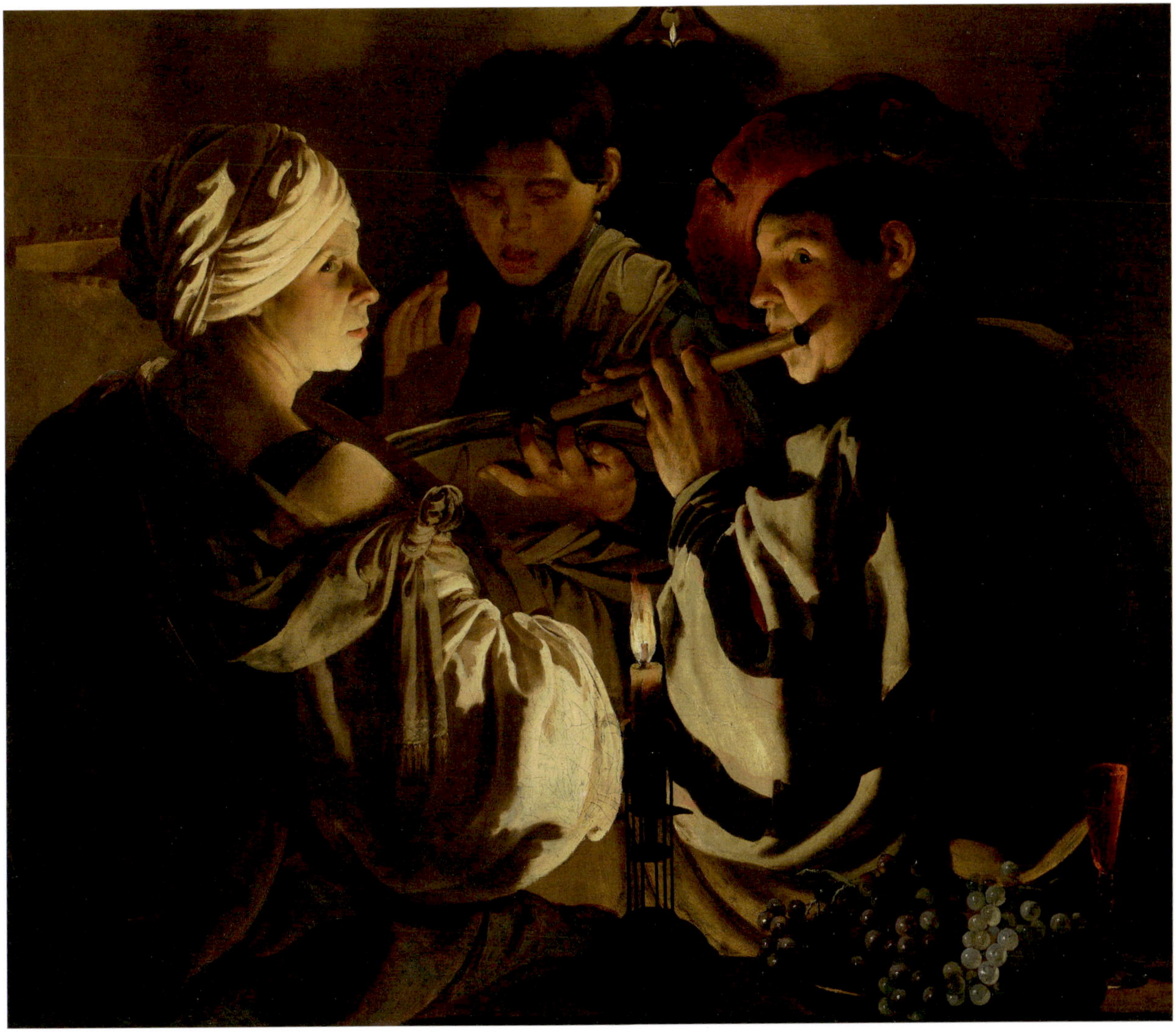

Pieter Saenredam

(1597–1665)

The Interior of the Grote Kerk at Haarlem, 1636–7

Oil on oak, 59.5 x 81.7 cm
Salting Bequest, 1910

Saenredam, who specialised in painting church interiors, produced a series of complex views of the Grote Kerk in Haarlem. Here, the low vantage point crops the foreground columns and most of the wooden ceiling vaulting. Denying a view of the church's upper reaches avoids complicated perspectival problems and suggests the monumentality of the space – giving the impression that the viewer is, like the carefully placed figures, tiny in relation to the columns. Saenredam's spare, light-filled spaces celebrate the simplicity of the Protestant aesthetic, which had stripped churches of 'idolatrous' Catholic imagery.

Possibly trained as an architect's draughtsman, Saenredam had a unique grasp of perspective that set him apart from his contemporaries. Taking advantage of recently published ground plans and elevations of the church, he pioneered a mathematical approach to architectural painting, developing on-site sketches into precise scale drawings that he traced onto the painting's panel support. His approach to documentation was as meticulous as his technique; although the painting itself is not signed or dated, on the preparatory design Saenredam refers to it as completed in May 1637.

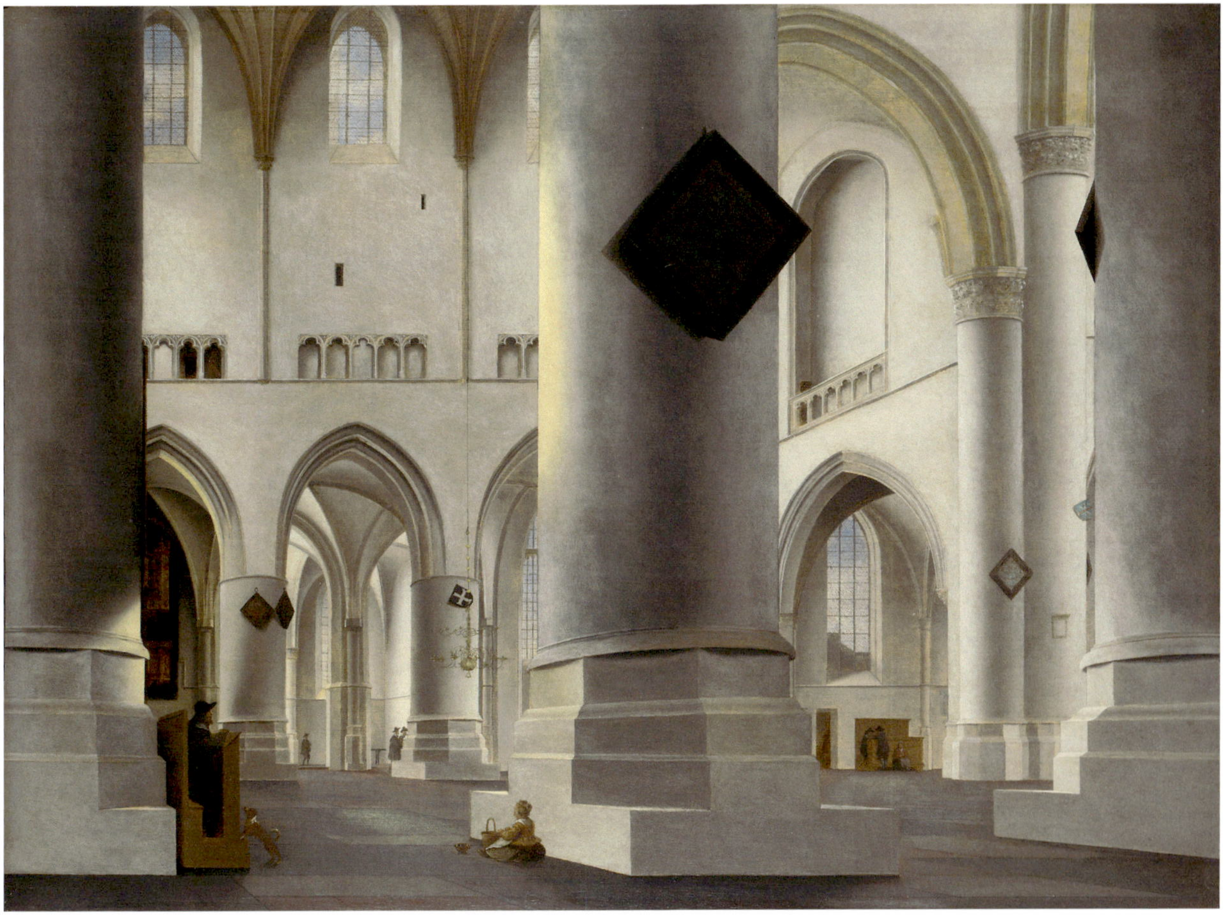

Harmen Steenwyck

(1612–1656)

Still Life: An Allegory of the Vanities of Human Life, about 1640

Oil on oak, 39.2 x 50.7 cm
Presented by Lord Savile, 1888

A shaft of clear light cascades from upper left to illuminate objects clustered at the corner of a table. The strongest light falls on a human skull, resting on a recorder and surrounded by a pocket watch, a shell, an extinguished oil lamp, a Japanese sword with inlaid scabbard, a lute, a large earthenware jug, several books, a shawm, and a wooden box flamboyantly inscribed with the artist's signature.

The skull's prominence indicates that the painting was intended as a *vanitas*, a reminder of the transience of human life. Other objects echo the theme (the smoking lamp, the watch) or allude to vain secular concerns. Yet Steenwyck goes beyond the rather heavy-handed moralising of his chosen subject to appeal to our senses. In this stark, luminous image, light creates a sense of atmosphere, while varied surface textures – rope, wood, earthenware, paper, silk, metal, bone – are juxtaposed to emphasise their unique properties. These rare and costly objects were not exclusively symbols of impending death, but also cherished tools and objectives of a diligent and active life on earth.

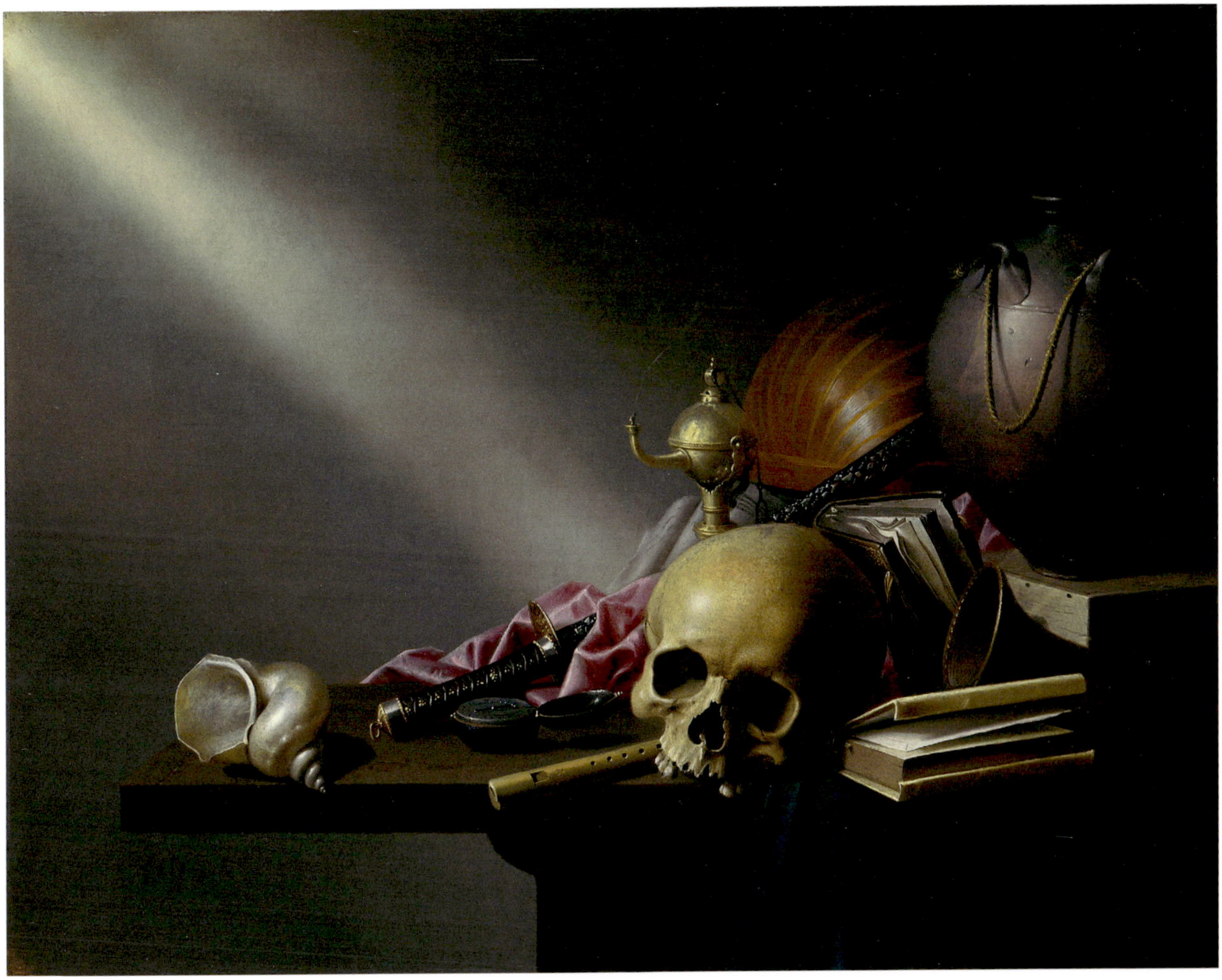

Thomas de Keyser

(1596/7–1667)

Portrait of Constantijn Huygens and his (?) Clerk, 1627

Oil on oak, 92.4 x 69.3 cm
Bequeathed by Richard Simmons, 1847

Constantijn Huygens (1596–1687), Lord of Zuylichem, was among the most powerful, influential and cosmopolitan figures of his age. He served as ambassador to Venice and England (where he was knighted by King James I in 1622), was secretary and advisor to three successive stadholders from the ruling House of Orange, and pursued a wide range of intellectual and artistic interests.

Huygens seems to have travelled specifically to Amsterdam from his home in The Hague to pose for this impressive portrait. De Keyser was the most successful portrait painter in Amsterdam during the 1620s, specialising in small full-length likenesses filled with detail. Here, he created a revealing image of a worldly statesman and intellectual of the seventeenth century. Fashionably dressed, Huygens turns gracefully to receive a letter from the clerk who stands respectfully at his side. The terrestrial and celestial globes, archlute, and drawings on the table refer to Huygens's interests in astronomy, music and architecture respectively, while the seascape over the fireplace reminds us of his interest in painting.

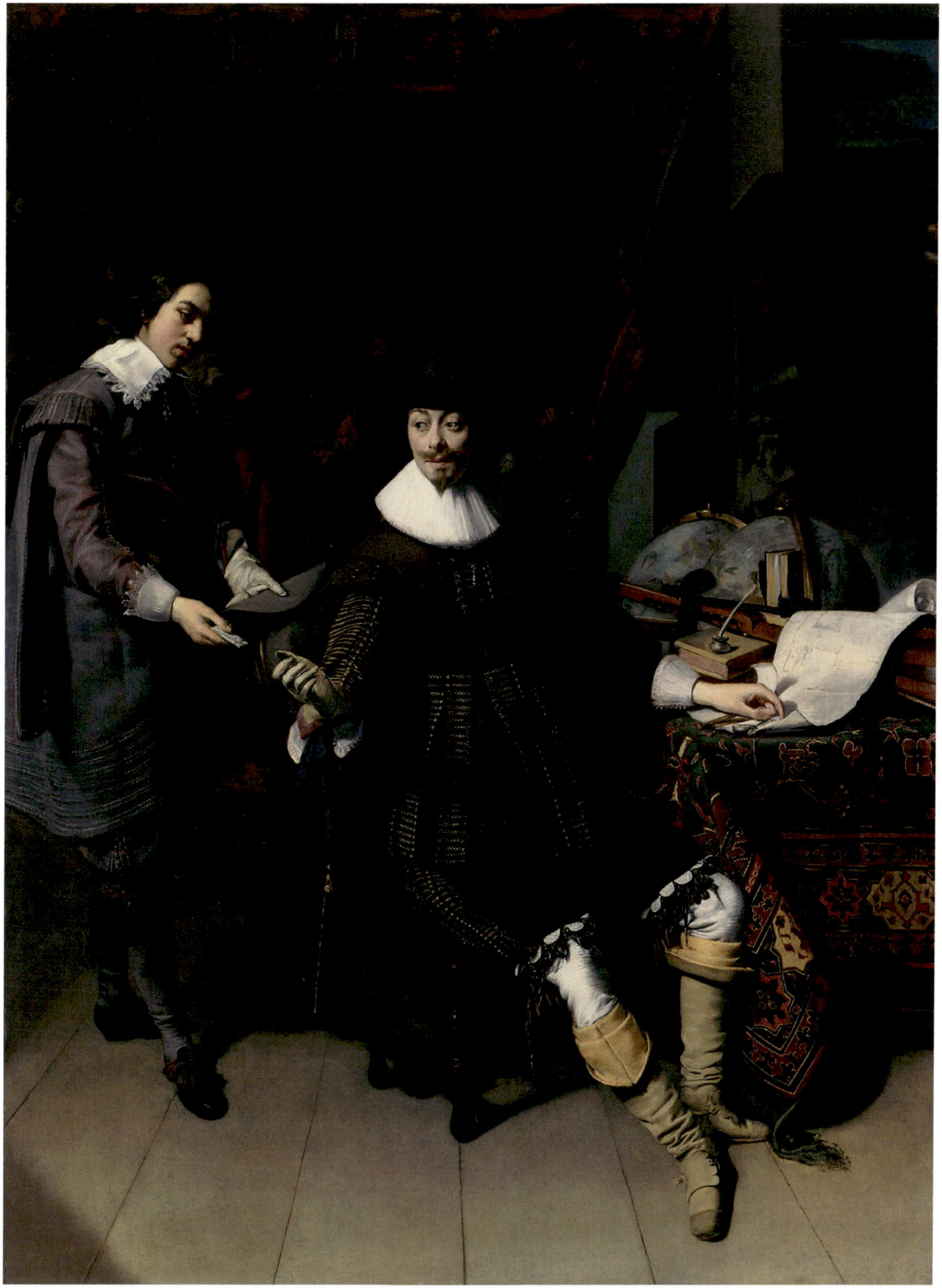

Gerard ter Borch

(1617–1681)

The Swearing of the Oath of Ratification of the Treaty of Münster, 1648

Oil on copper, 45.4 x 58.5 cm
Presented by Sir Richard Wallace, 1871

The Treaty of Münster brought an end to the Thirty Years' War (1618–48) in the German territories and the Eighty Years' War (1568–1648) between the Spanish and the Dutch; with the signing, the Dutch Republic was finally recognised as an independent country. Three years of negotiations preceded this momentous event, involving diplomats from Spain, the Netherlands, Germany, Italy, France and Sweden. Though modern opinions of the Treaty's significance vary, it remains a remarkable statement of internationalism and religious tolerance.

Ter Borch lived in the German city of Münster for over two years and witnessed much of the work that preceded the ratification. He painted individual portraits of several delegates and their families, but the pinnacle of his achievement is this detailed image, the only painted depiction of the event. The work is highly factual: the wealth of visual information confers solemn significance. The most important signatories of the Treaty are at the centre: the Dutch delegates are to the left; the Spanish to the right. At the far left Ter Borch inserted his self-portrait, a traditional device intended to proclaim the artist as an eye-witness.

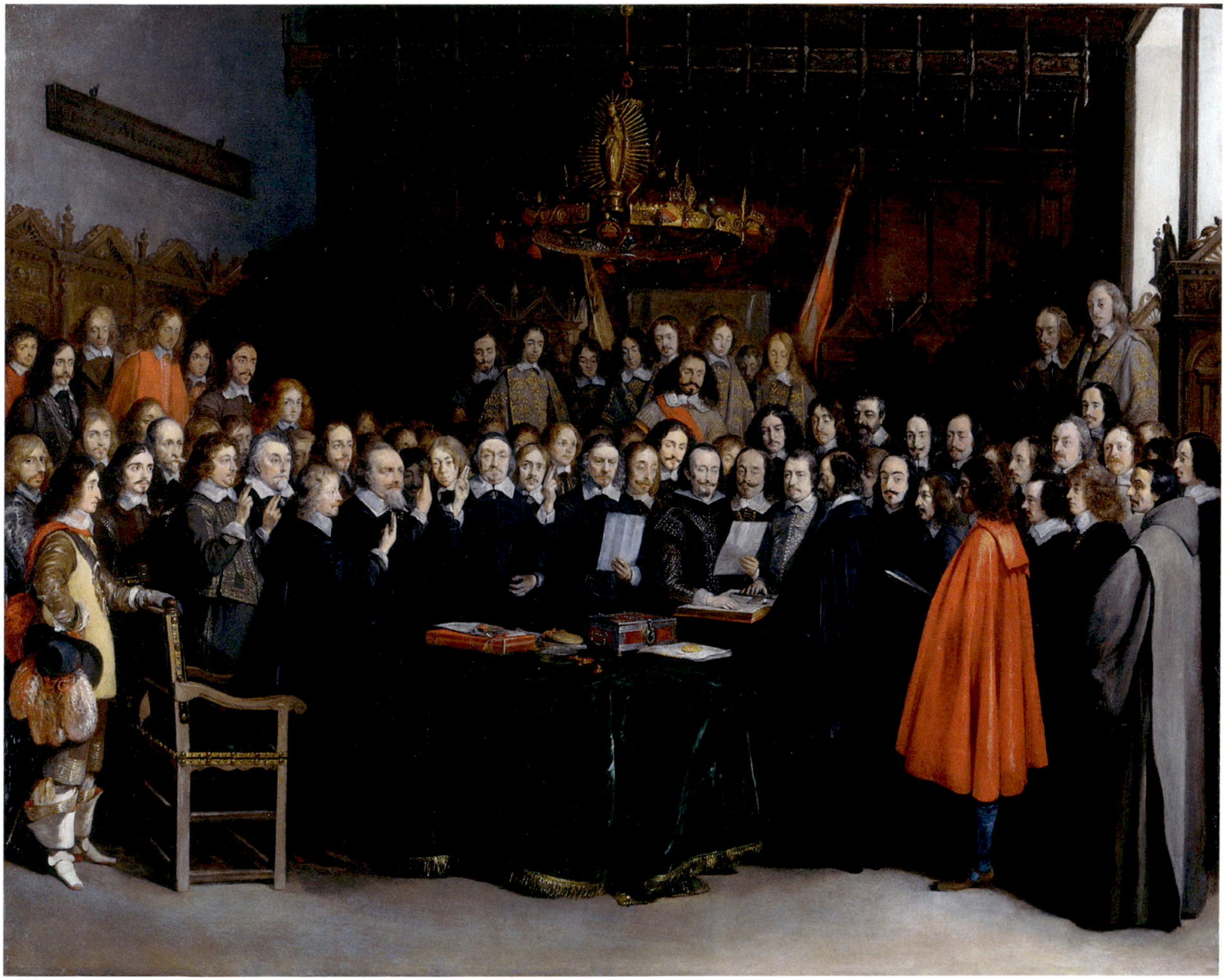

Rembrandt

(1606–1669)

Belshazzar's Feast, about 1636–8

Oil on canvas, 167.6 x 209.2 cm
Bought with a contribution from The Art Fund, 1964

This dramatic scene from the Old Testament book of Daniel (5: 1–31) is a powerful example of Rembrandt's inventive approach to historical subjects. The Babylonian king Belshazzar had been feasting using the sacred vessels looted by his father, Nebuchadnezzar, from the Temple of Jerusalem. Frozen in horror, he and his guests look on as a disembodied hand inscribes cryptic letters in a nimbus of light on the palace wall. Only Daniel could interpret the Hebrew letters, which foretell the division of the Kingdom and Belshazzar's death that night: 'God hath numbered thy kingdom and finished it ... Thou art weighed in the balances, and art found wanting ... Thy kingdom is divided'. Belshazzar spins around in fear, knocking over a golden chalice and causing one of his guests to recoil into our space.

History painting was highly prized in the seventeenth century, and Rembrandt's combination of close-up views, dramatic lighting and intense realism revolutionised the genre. Although depictions of Belshazzar's Feast were rare, it was occasionally used to decorate dining rooms, warning against overindulgence and the misuse of sacred objects. The unusual subject makes the most of Rembrandt's skill as a painter of light and its effects: the divine light illuminates the richness and texture of Belshazzar's costume, the wine and his illicit booty.

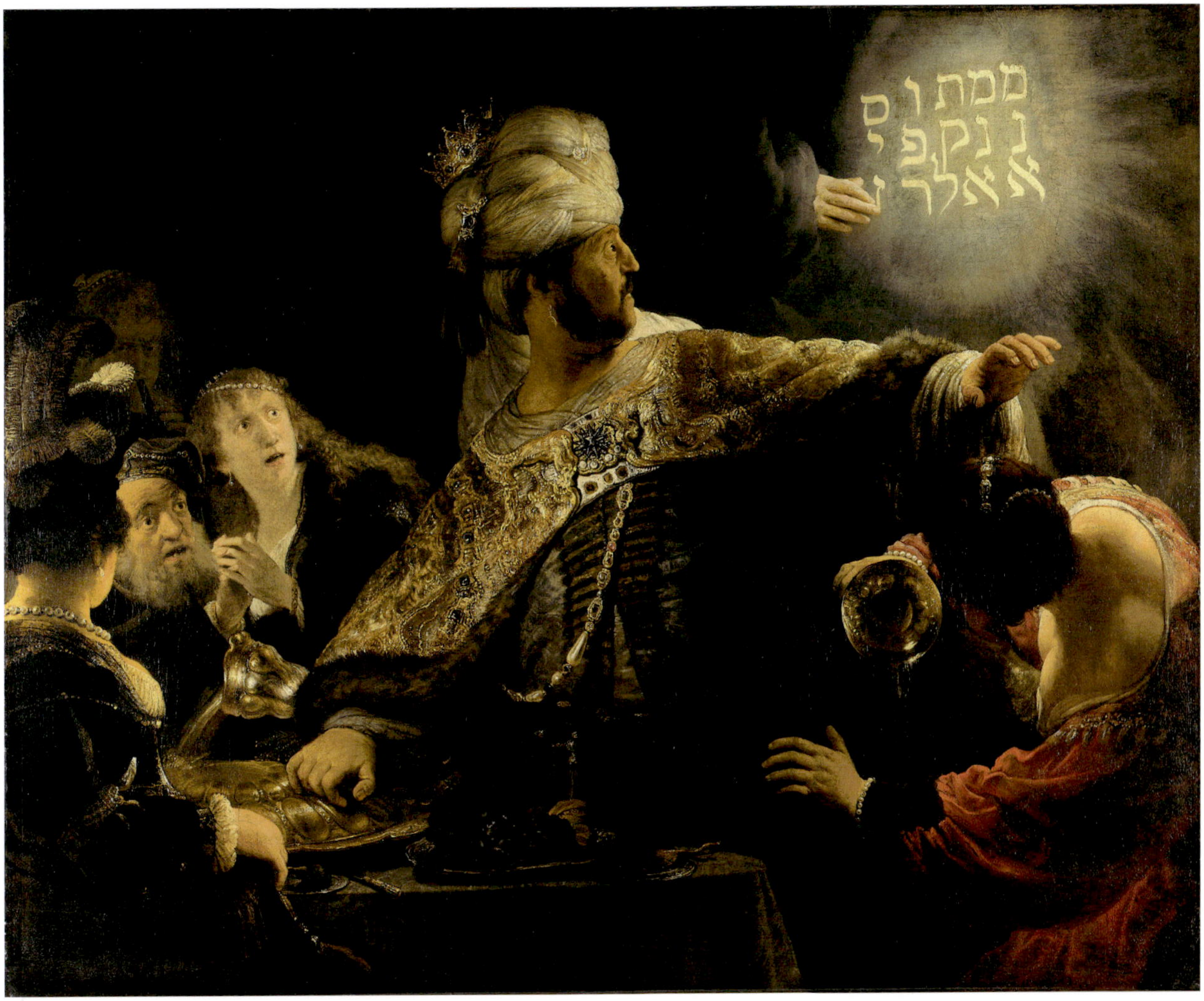

Rembrandt

(1606–1669)

Self Portrait at the Age of 34, 1640

Oil on canvas, 102 x 80 cm

Rembrandt painted, etched or drew more than 70 self portraits during his career, an extraordinary series that records for posterity the artist's appearance from his youthful days in Leiden to his final years in Amsterdam (p. 55). This striking work shows Rembrandt at his most distinguished, a visual proclamation of his success as one of Amsterdam's most fashionable painters.

The strong pyramidal composition and the self-assured pose are derived from well-known portraits by sixteenth-century masters such as Raphael, Titian, Lucas van Leyden and Albrecht Dürer. By evoking these references, Rembrandt drew an ambitious parallel between his own talents and those of revered artists of the past; and between his social status and that of the aristocratic subjects of these earlier portraits. The fabulously opulent costume – also inspired by sixteenth-century dress – showcases Rembrandt's ability to suggest the varied textures of materials.

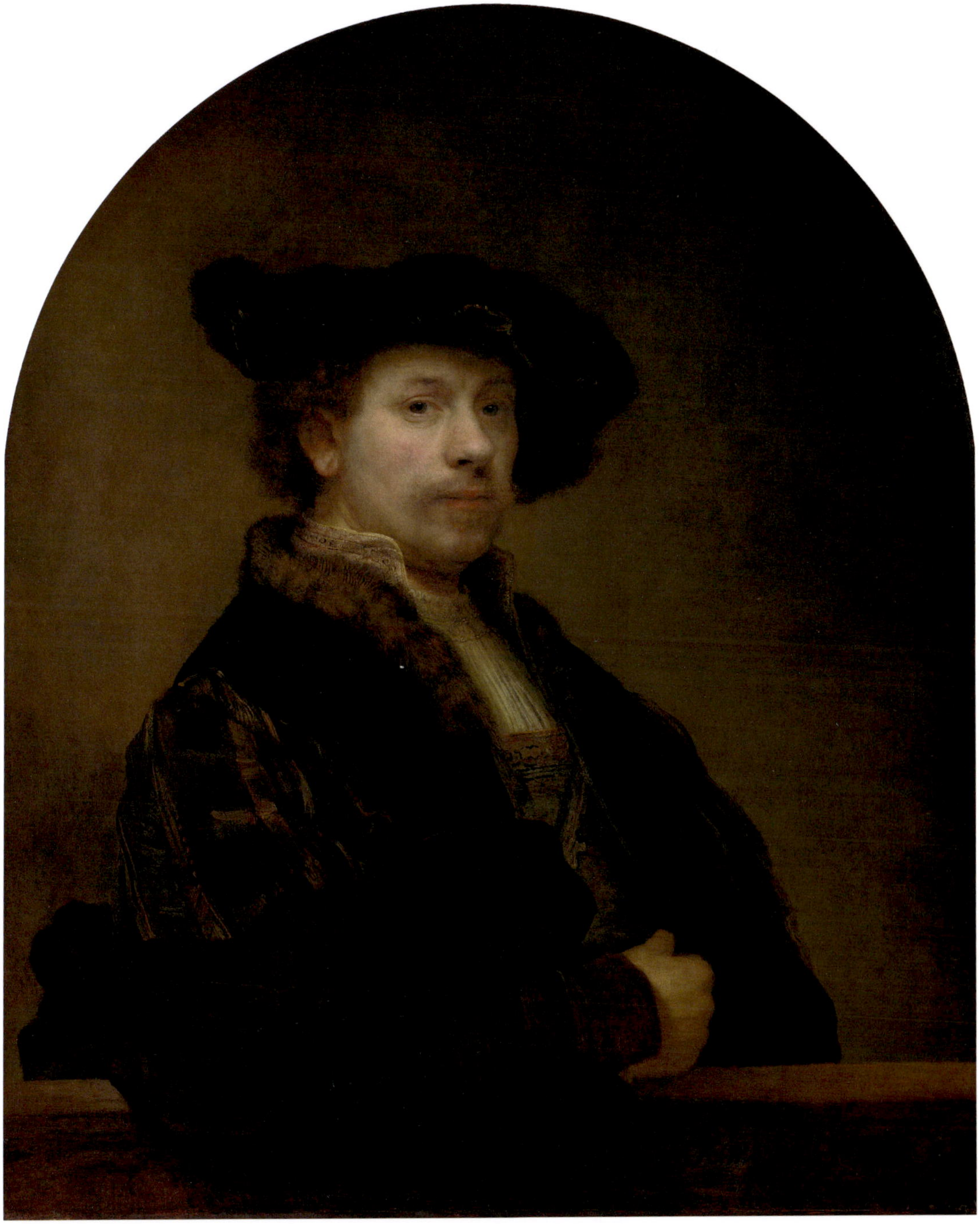

Carel Fabritius

(1622–1654)

A Young Man in a Fur Cap and a Cuirass (probably a Self Portrait), 1654

Oil on canvas, 70.5 x 61.5 cm

A young man dressed in a soldier's cuirass and fur cap stares intently out of the picture. His frank gaze suggests self-examination, while his features bear a strong similarity to other paintings by the artist regarded as self-portraits. Shortly after this likeness was painted, in October 1654, Fabritius was killed when a gunpowder store exploded in Delft.

Fabritius is regarded as Rembrandt's most talented pupil, perhaps borrowing from him the idea of showing himself in three-quarter pose and military dress in a portrait or *tronie*. *Tronies* were individual anonymous head studies, made either for sale or as practice pieces, and Fabritius's self-portrait could belong to this genre. Like his teacher, Fabritius altered his brushwork to describe different textures – here the thick white highlights of the cuirass contrast with the thin, delicate brushstrokes used to attain the precise finish of the skin. The clarity of the portrait is enhanced by diffuse daylight that reveals the nuances of every surface. The shaded backdrop allows Fabritius's face to shine out, while his torso is set in relief against the lighter portion.

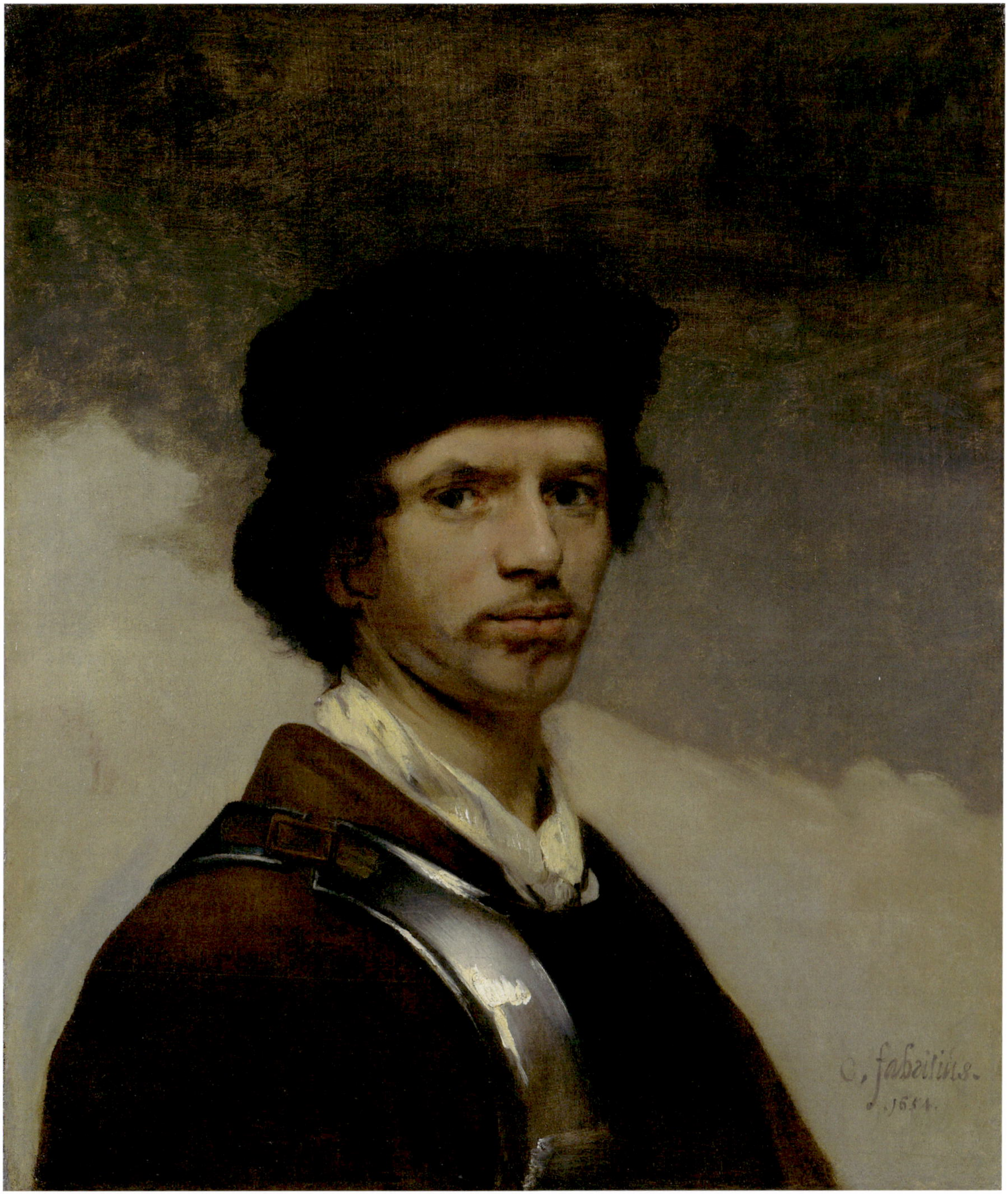
C. fabritius.
.1654.

Carel Fabritius

(1622–1654)

A View of Delft, with a Musical Instrument Seller's Stall, 1652

Oil on canvas, 15.5 x 31.7 cm
Presented by The Art Fund, 1922

Fabritius was admired as a painter of 'perspectives', or illusionistic architectural views: the artist and theorist Samuel van Hoogstraten (p. 44) wrote that Fabritius's perspectives 'excited wonder and amazement'. This diminutive painting is the only one of these celebrated views to have survived. It depicts a corner in Delft looking towards the Nieuwe Kerk from the southeast. To the left is a musical instrument-maker's stall, with a man seated by a ledge.

The most striking aspect of this enigmatic painting is the distorted perspective: the church appears too small, the instruments thrust powerfully, even awkwardly into our space, and the street expands into a sea of cobblestones. It seems likely that the canvas was mounted on a curved concave support and placed at the rear of a triangular perspective box, with a peephole at the opposite angle. When viewed in this way, objects appear in proportion to each other and shadows fall correctly. Fabritius's ingenious composition was part of an ongoing fascination with optics and perspective that inspired numerous Dutch artists in the seventeenth century.

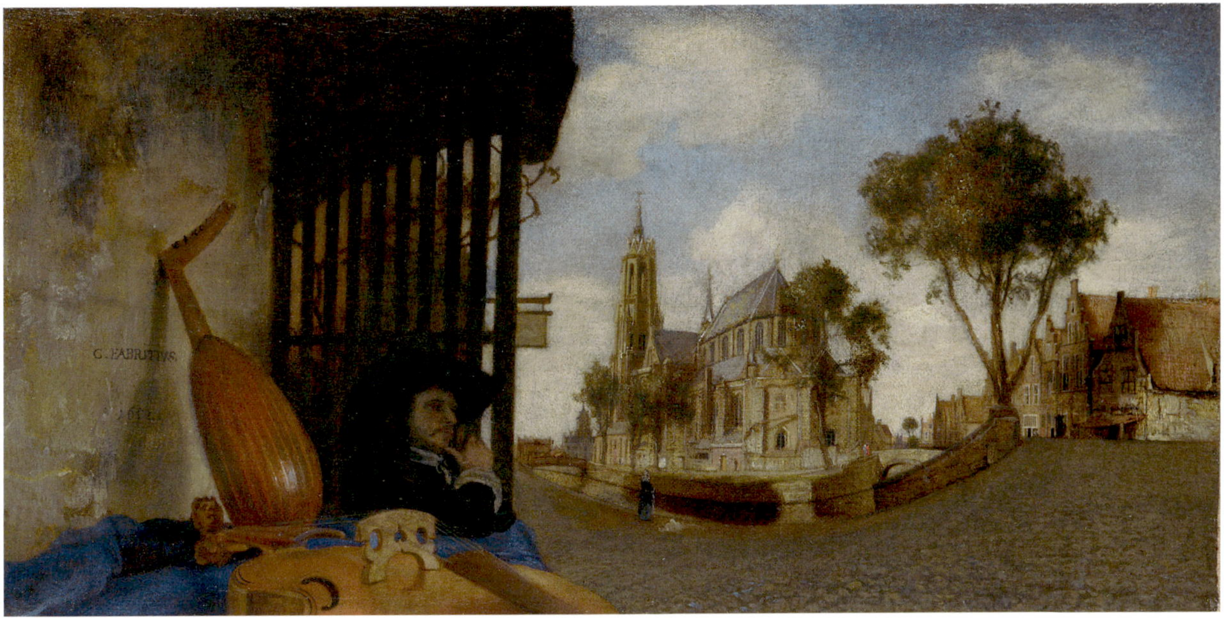
C. FABRITIVS

Samuel van Hoogstraten

(1627–1678)

A Peepshow with Views of the Interior of a Dutch House, about 1655–60

Oil and egg on wood, 58 x 88 x 60.5 cm
Presented by Sir Robert and Lady Witt through The Art Fund, 1924

Hoogstraten's perspective box is one of only six surviving examples of this popular seventeenth-century 'curiosity'. Painted inside and out, it has two openings through which the viewer 'peeps' into an imaginary Dutch interior provided with all the comforts of an upper-middle-class home. Windows and doorways offer intriguing views into adjoining spaces. Objects that appear in the centre of the room – chairs, the broom, the dog – are actually painted on the flat walls of the box. When properly viewed from the peepholes, their distorted shapes fall into alignment, producing a convincing illusion of three dimensions.

Hoogstraten, a theorist as well as a painter, considered the perspective box's mix of painting, artifice and the science of optics to be an admirable demonstration of painting's aims. An ideal painting, he felt, 'makes things that do not exist appear to exist and thus deceives in a permissible, pleasurable, and praiseworthy manner'. The perspective box contains explicit references to the artist's pride in his achievement. Its exterior is decorated with allegorical images of creation, and of the three incentives that motivated an artist: love of art, love of wealth and love of fame.

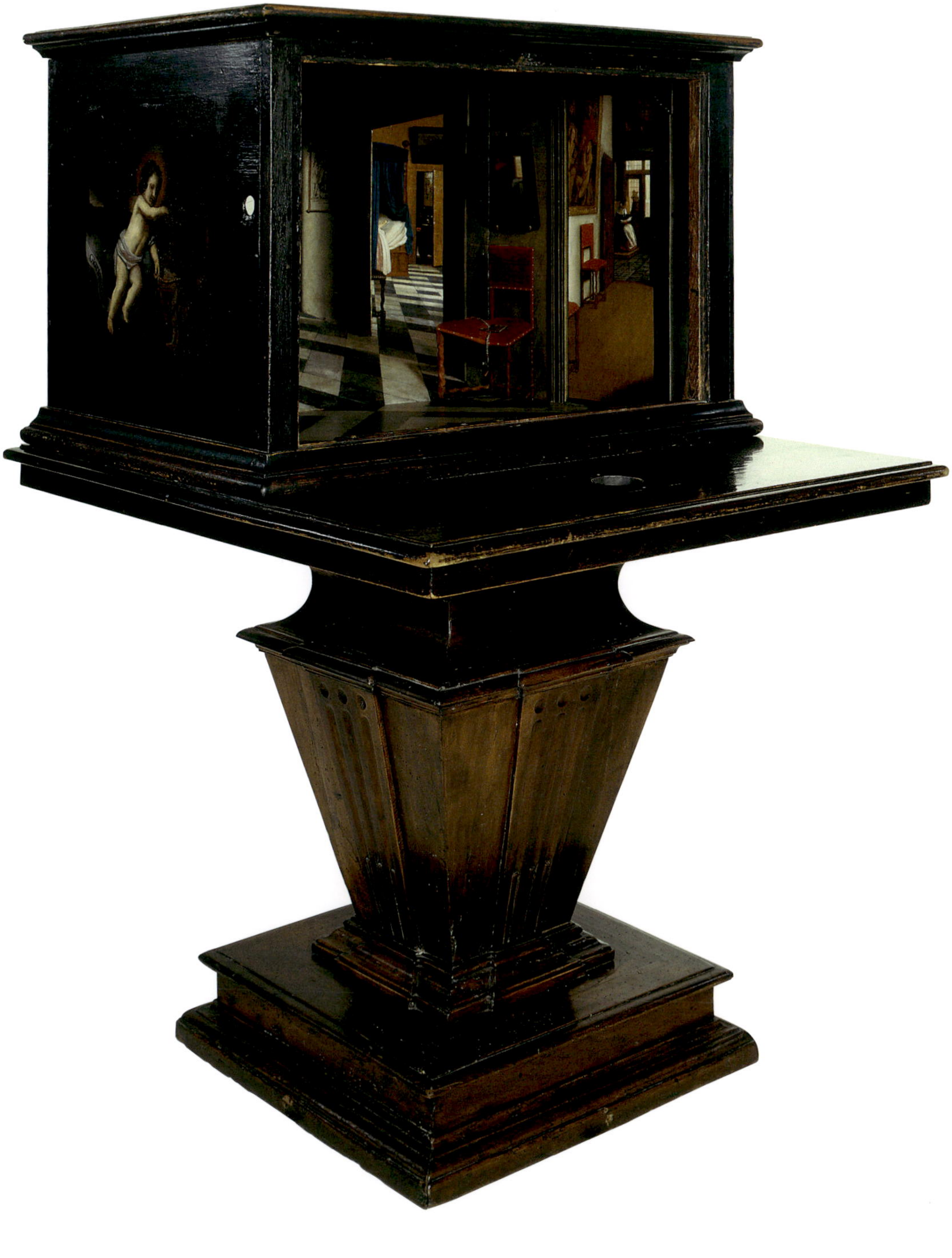

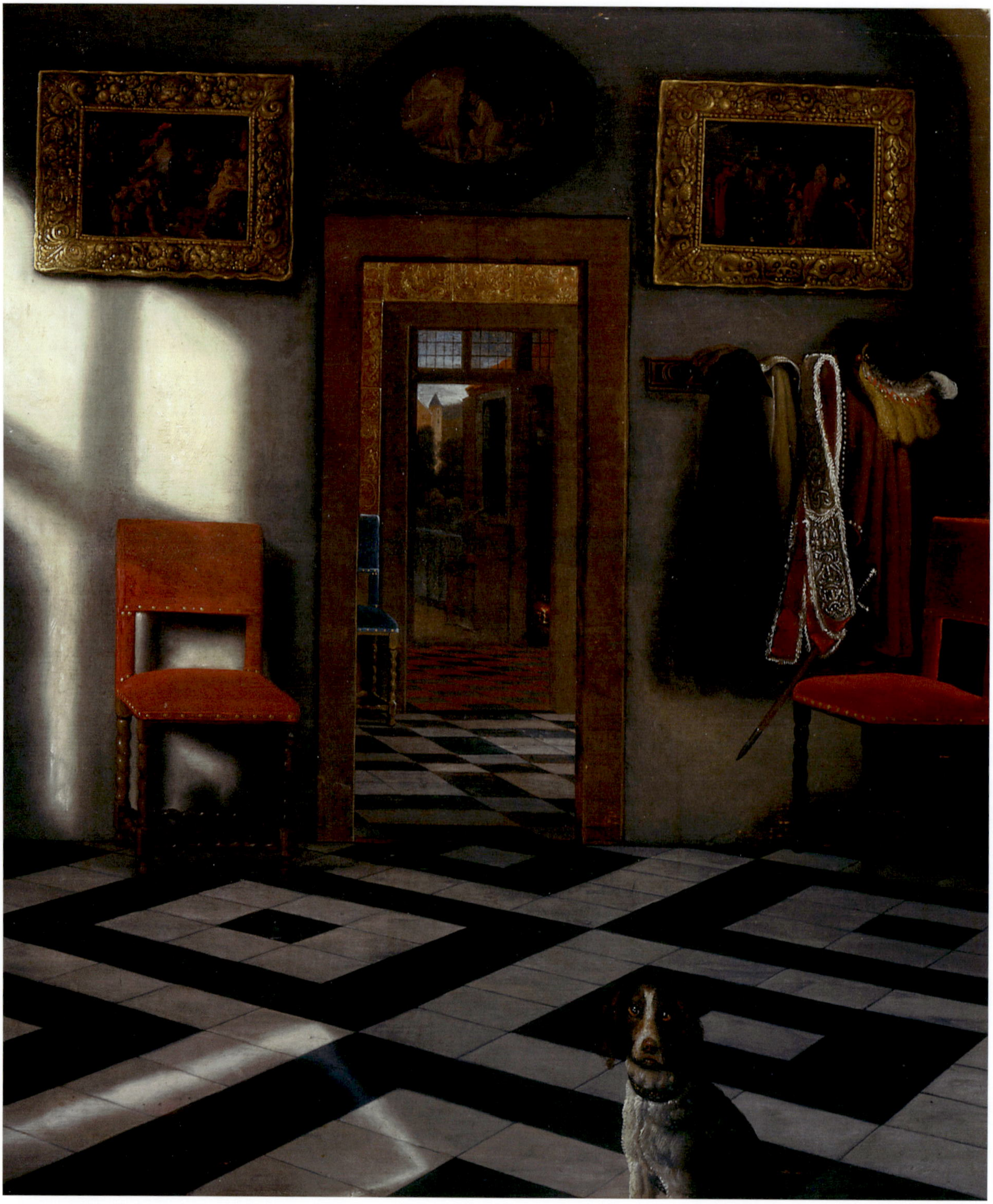

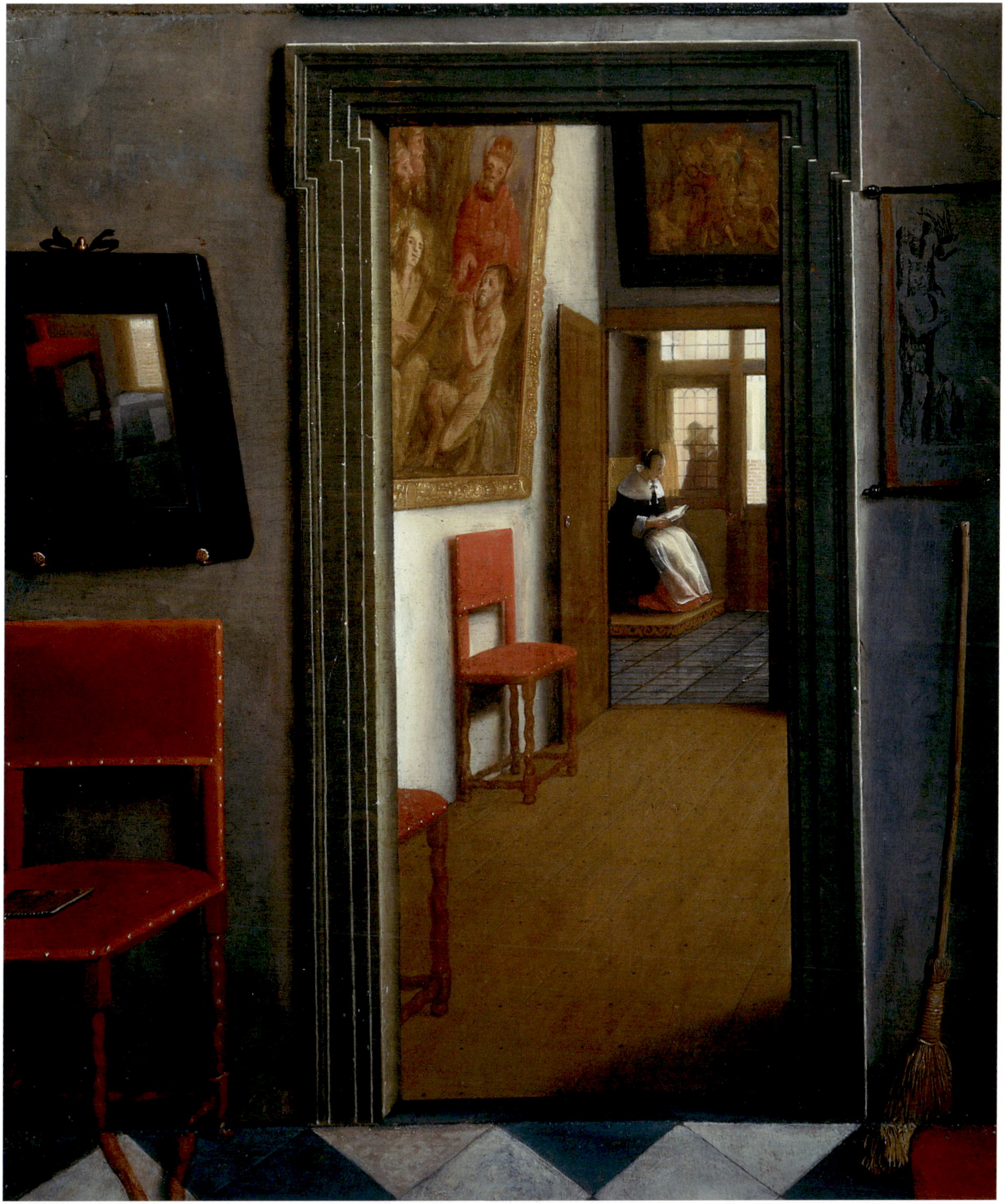

Pieter de Hooch

(1629–1684)

The Courtyard of a House in Delft, 1658

Oil on canvas, 73.5 x 60 cm
Purchased with the Peel collection, 1871

Glowing in the afternoon sun, a herringbone pattern of pale yellow bricks welcomes the viewer into the courtyard of this Delft home, where a maid tenderly instructs her young charge in household duties. The mistress of the house looks out from an interior corridor onto the street, or perhaps even into the window of the house opposite. The shiny tiled walls and spotless flagstones of her domain contrast with the rough brickwork of the maid's outdoor realm.

De Hooch was innovative as a painter of homely domestic subjects, and here he juxtaposes the shadowy, spartan interior of the home with the overgrown trellis and ramshackle shed in the sunny courtyard. The sensitive portrayal of utilitarian architecture and mundane objects, and views through domestic spaces, recall the Dutch fascination with perspective boxes (pp. 45–7). The inscription on the plaque above the doorway exhorts tranquility and humility, sentiments in keeping with the mood of the scene.

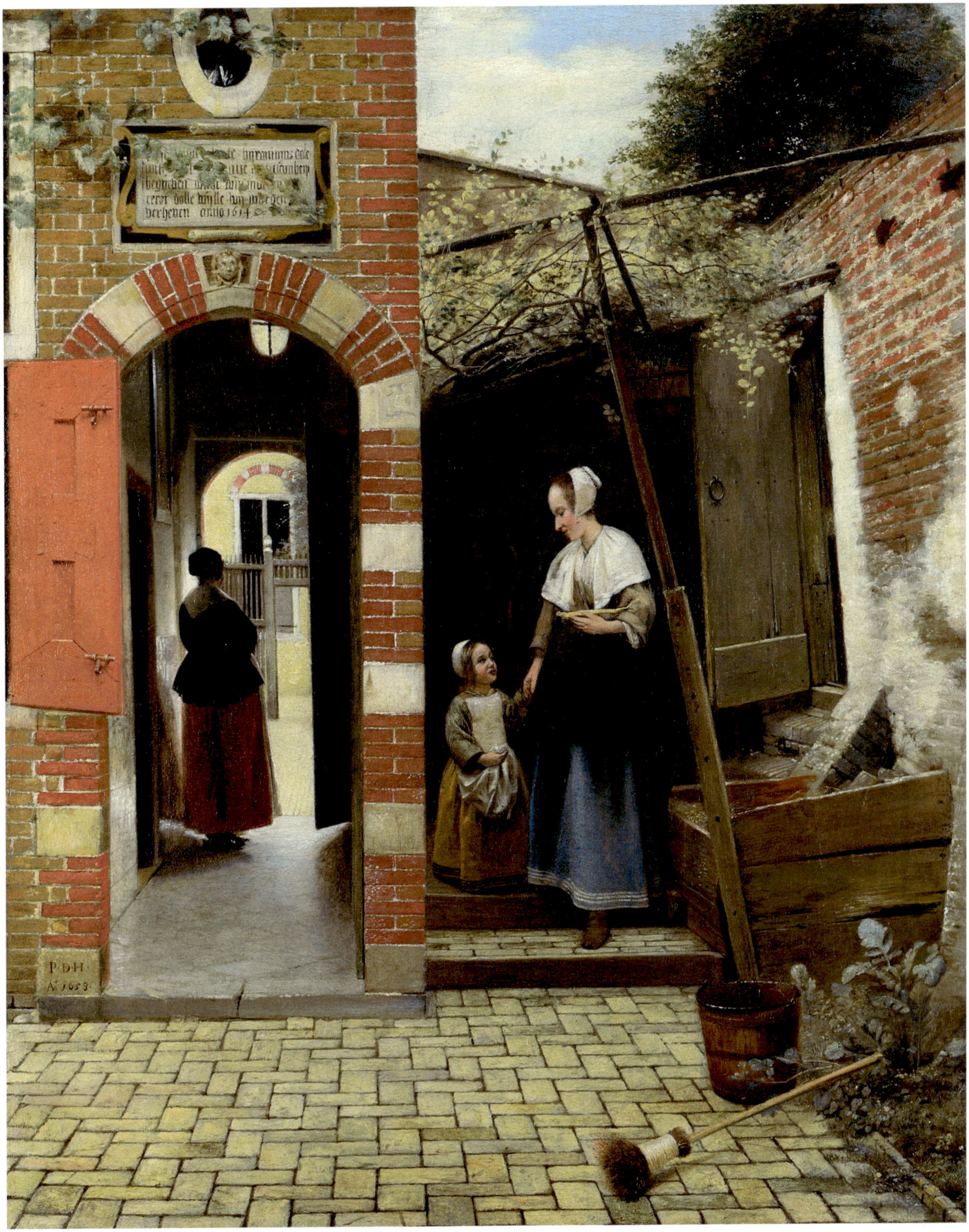
P·D·H·
A° 1658

Gerard ter Borch

(1617–1681)

An Officer dictating a Letter, about 1655–8

Oil on canvas, 74.5 x 51 cm
Bequeathed by Mrs M. V. James from the Arthur James collection, 1948

Ter Borch's appreciation for the minutiae of everyday life made him not only a brilliant portraitist (p. 35), but also one of the most innovative genre painters of the seventeenth century. He was particularly adept at expressing the delicate, often precarious, relationships between the sexes: the thrill of burgeoning love in an era when courtships were carefully proscribed, chaperoned and (among the wealthy bourgeoisie, at least) conducted in painstaking consultation with published etiquette manuals.

Genre scenes of officers reading or receiving military despatches were common in Dutch painting, but here the domestic setting and accessories suggest that Ter Borch's officers are engaged in writing not a military brief, but a love letter. The young officer at left pauses as he writes; his companion appears to be dictating to him. Is he helping his friend find the perfect words? Gazing directly at the viewer, the trumpeter at right waits patiently – with a somewhat wry expression – to carry the letter away. Characteristic of Ter Borch's attention to detail, the hem of his blue jerkin is frayed where his sword has rubbed against it.

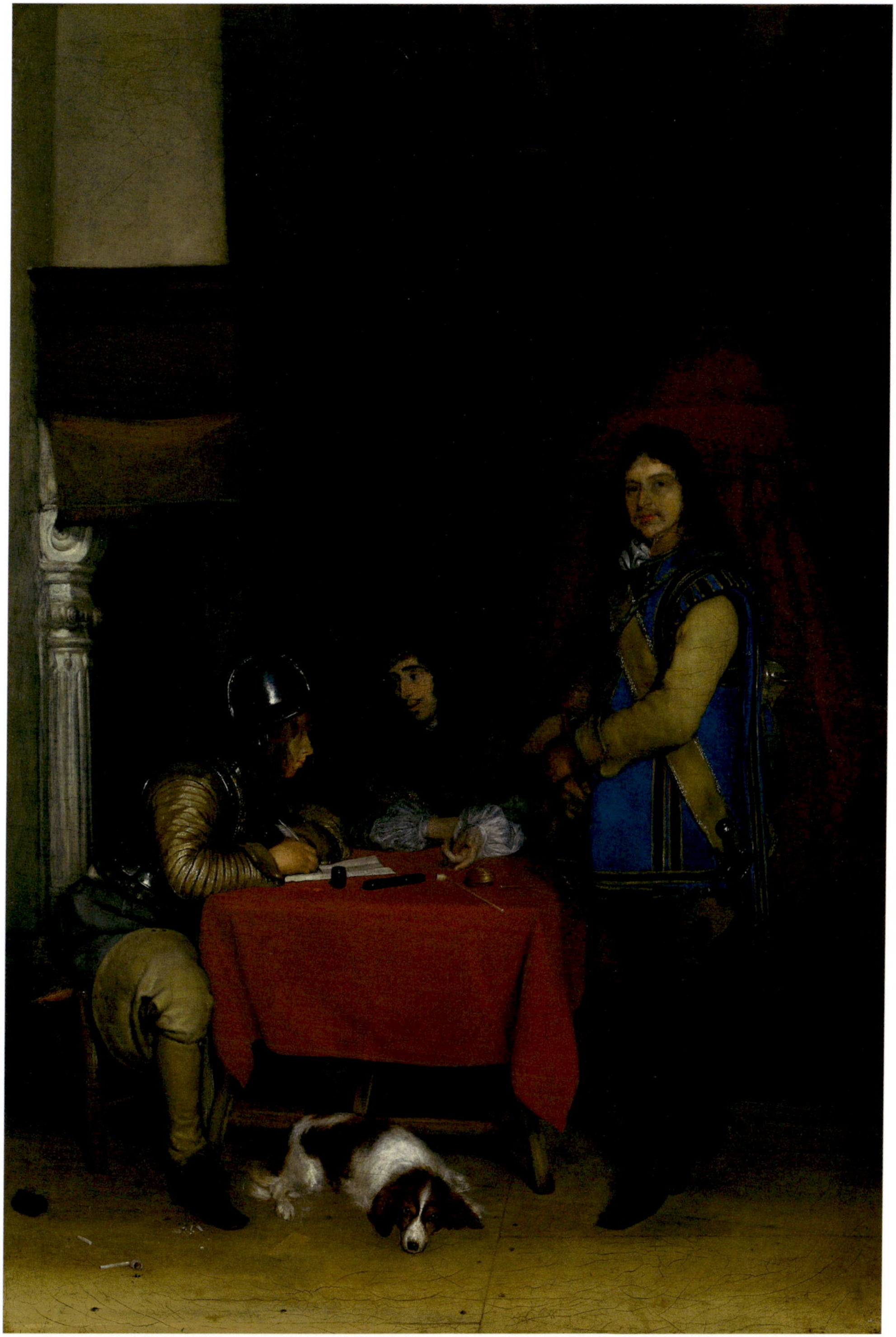

Rembrandt

(1606–1669)

A Woman bathing in a Stream (Hendrickje Stoffels?), 1654

Oil on oak, 61.8 x 47 cm
Holwell Carr Bequest, 1831

Rembrandt's beloved first wife, Saskia van Uylenburgh, died in 1642. A few years later, in 1647, Hendrickje Stoffels joined the household as housekeeper and soon became the painter's mistress. Although they never married – indeed, in the year this picture was painted, Hendrickje was denounced by the Church for 'practising whoredom with the painter Rembrandt' – she became his second great love.

Although no documented portraits of Hendrickje are known, this is among several works from the early 1650s thought to represent her; the palpable affection and informality certainly suggests an intimacy between painter and model. The work's small size and unfinished appearance might suggest that it is a sketch for some larger work, yet Rembrandt considered it complete enough to sign. The loose linen shift is not only highly erotic but also one of the most stunning examples of Rembrandt's virtuoso handling of paint. The lyrical vision of feminine sensuality is enriched by the sensual visual appeal of Rembrandt's painterly technique.

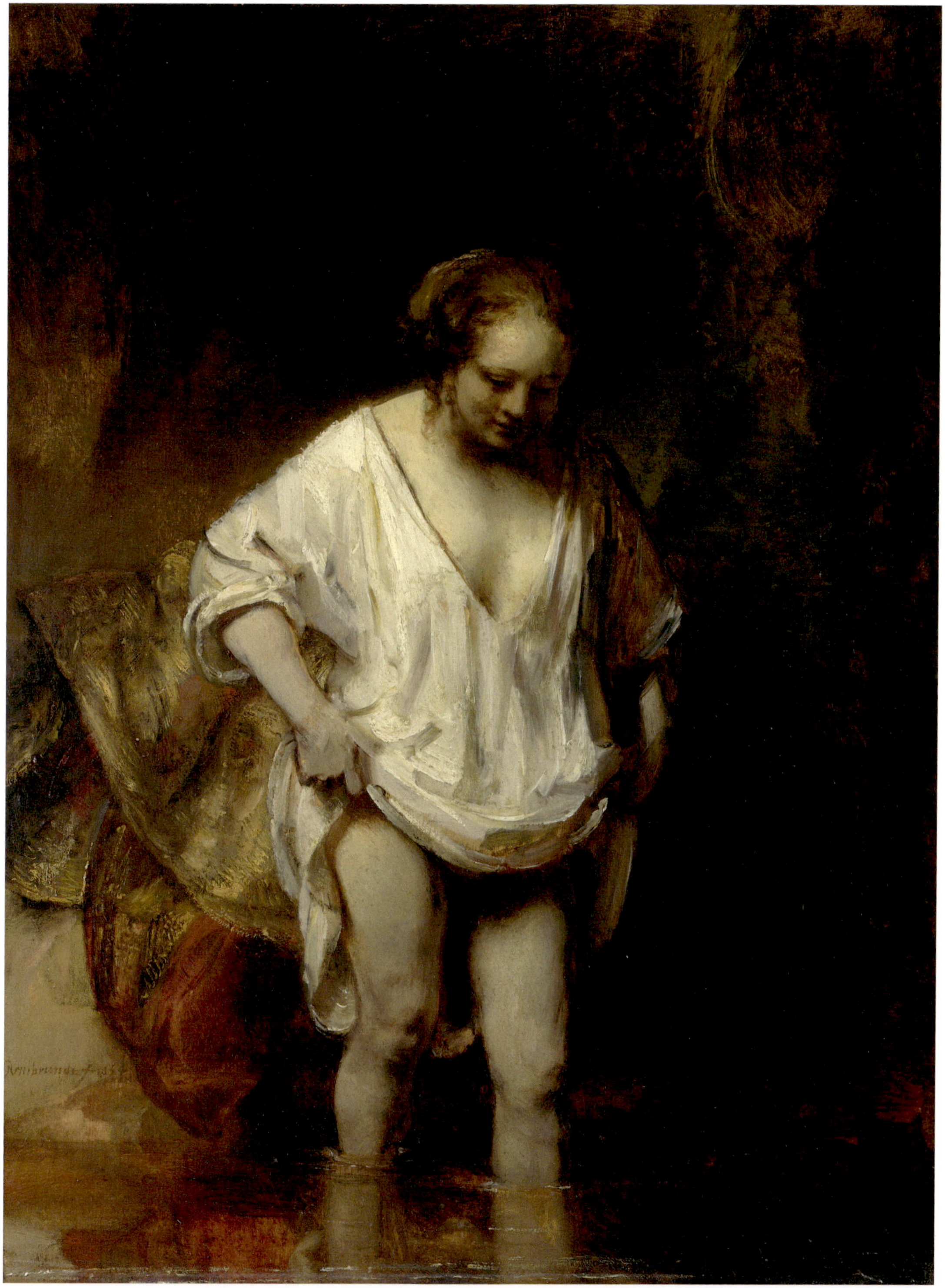

Rembrandt

(1606–1669)

Self Portrait at the Age of 63, 1669

Oil on canvas, 86 x 70.5 cm

Rembrandt continued painting self portraits until he died, relentlessly recording the effects of age, professional vicissitudes and personal tragedy upon his own visage. These remarkably forthright self-examinations are among the most moving paintings of the seventeenth century. Though the flesh of his face sags in loose crêpey folds, Rembrandt regards the viewer with an alert and level gaze. Wispy grey hair strays from beneath a tight-fitting cap or turban, a poignant approximation of the bushy locks seen in the more dashing earlier *Self Portrait* (p. 39). Here, too, Rembrandt's clothing bears no relation to contemporary fashions; the high-necked doublet reflects the working garb of fifteenth-century Netherlandish painters.

This powerful painting shows how Rembrandt masterfully manipulated technique to direct the viewer's attention within his compositions. Paint is applied most thickly to the face, turban and collar, giving these areas an impression of texture and rounded form. The turban's smooth white band was formed with broad horizontal strokes, while an astonishing variety of marks – dabbing, twisting and dragging the paint – suggest the rough texture of aged flesh.

Paulus Potter

(1625–1654)

Cattle and Sheep in a Stormy Landscape, 1647

Oil on oak, 46.3 x 37.8 cm
Salting Bequest, 1910

Although Potter's career was cut tragically short by his early death, his closely observed and minutely detailed images had a great impact on the development of Dutch animal and landscape painting. Animals are the principal players in his paintings, a reminder of the crucial role of livestock cultivation in the Netherlands during the early modern period. Indeed, dairy farming was key to seventeenth-century Dutch economic success, and the cow came to symbolise Dutch prosperity and well-being.

As one of the first Dutch painters to depict stormy landscapes, Potter employed dramatic alterations of yellow sunlight and dark, ominous clouds, as well as details such as wind-tossed trees, to convey the violence of a passing squall. Oddly, the animals seem unfazed by the vagaries of the weather. Only the young bull, poised in bold silhouette against the sky, seems energised – but whether by storm or the viewer's approach is difficult to say. Like so many of Potter's animals, the bull is depicted with a distinctive and charmingly portrait-like character.

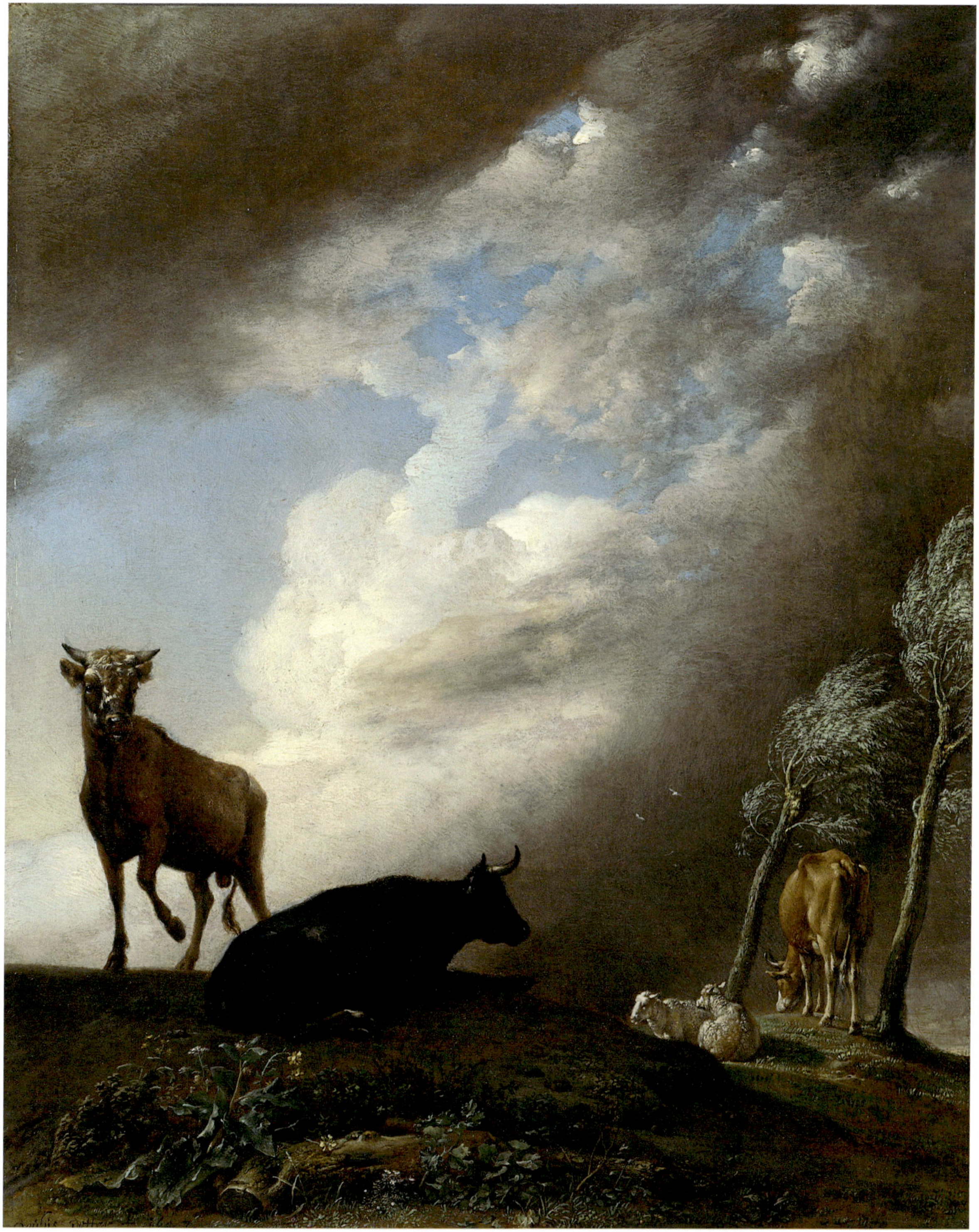

Jan Both

(about 1615–1652)

A Rocky Italian Landscape with Herdsmen and Muleteers, about 1645

Oil on canvas, 103 x 125 cm
Wynn Ellis Bequest, 1876

Although our eye is drawn to the travellers drinking from a spring in a rocky mountain pass, the real subject here is the rugged Roman countryside. Both was among the second generation of Dutch artists who went to Rome in the 1630s. Earlier artists such as Honthorst and Ter Brugghen (see pp. 22 and 26) visited the city to study the work of Caravaggio, but Both drew inspiration from the topography, ancient ruins and picturesque inhabitants of the Eternal City. His compositional devices and warm, naturalistic depiction of Italianate light exerted a huge impact on the next generation of Dutch landscapists – including Aelbert Cuyp (p. 62), who never visited Italy.

The composition is divided diagonally, contrasting the golden sky at dawn with the dark, densely wooded mountainside. As the sun is still low, only the uppermost leaves of the bushes, the silvery jade moss on the tree trunks and the cascading spring water are highlighted as they are touched by the light. Both used short, rough brushstrokes in muted colours to suggest forms such as leaves and bark; the lack of clarity reflects the hazy atmosphere.

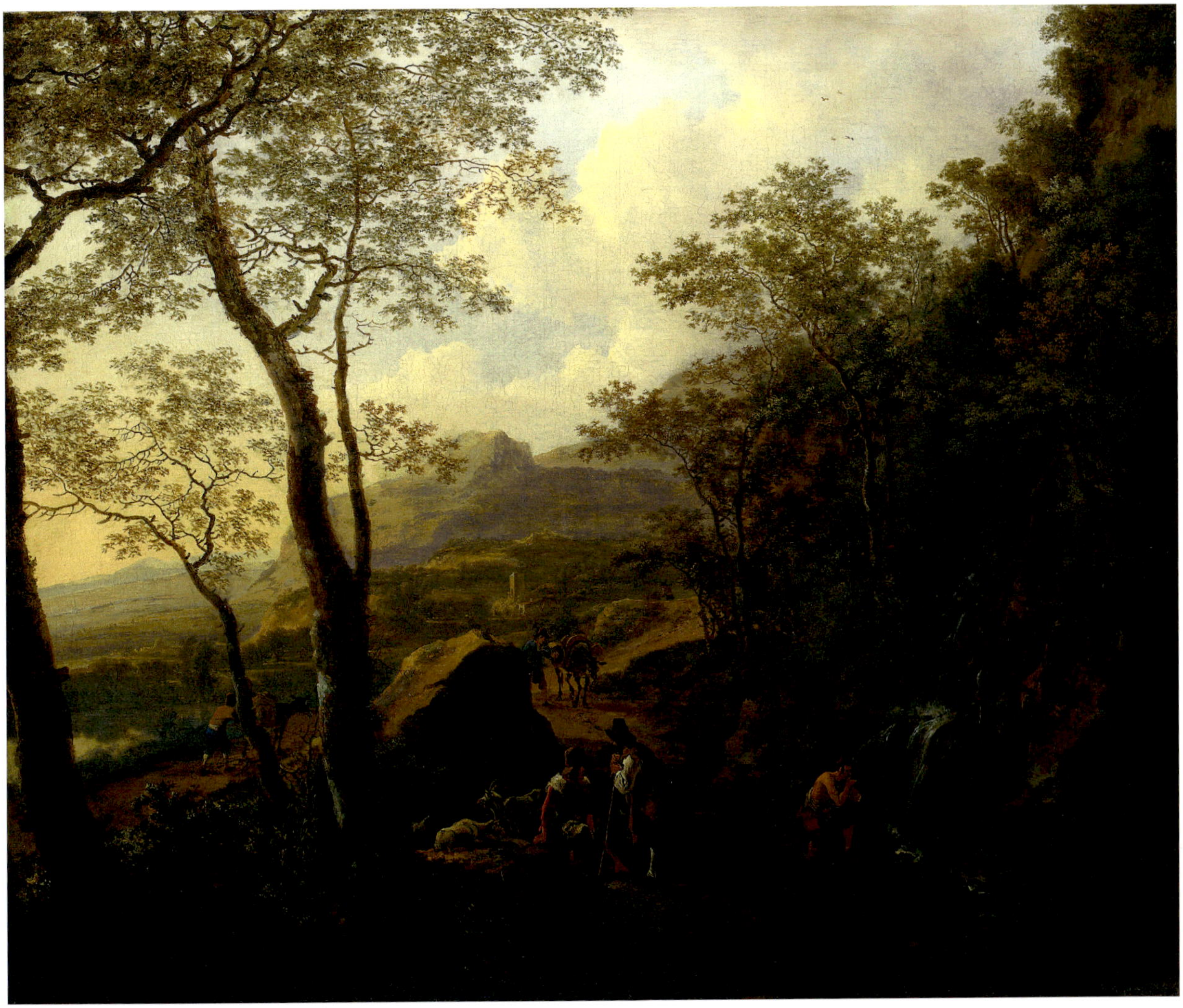

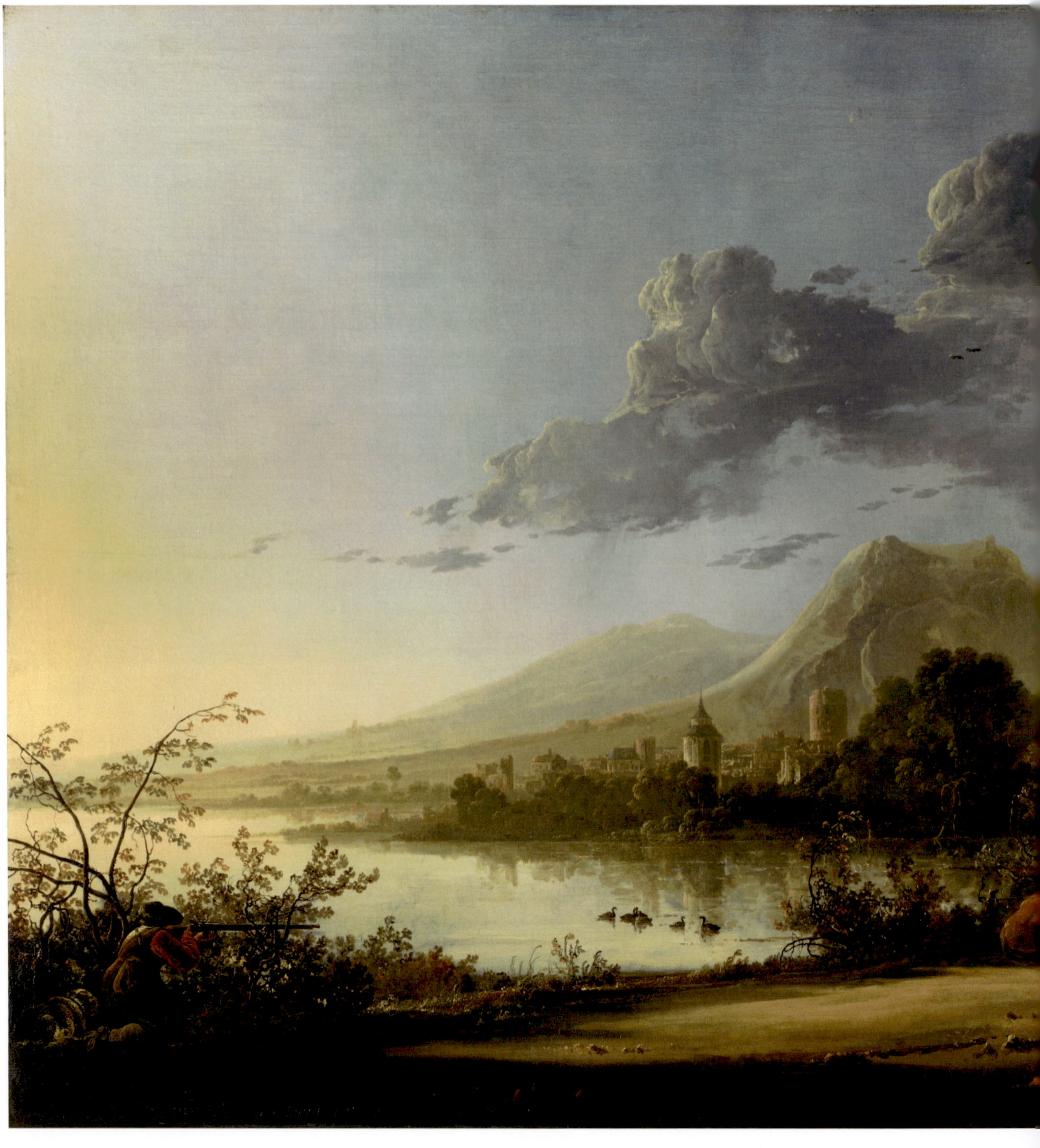

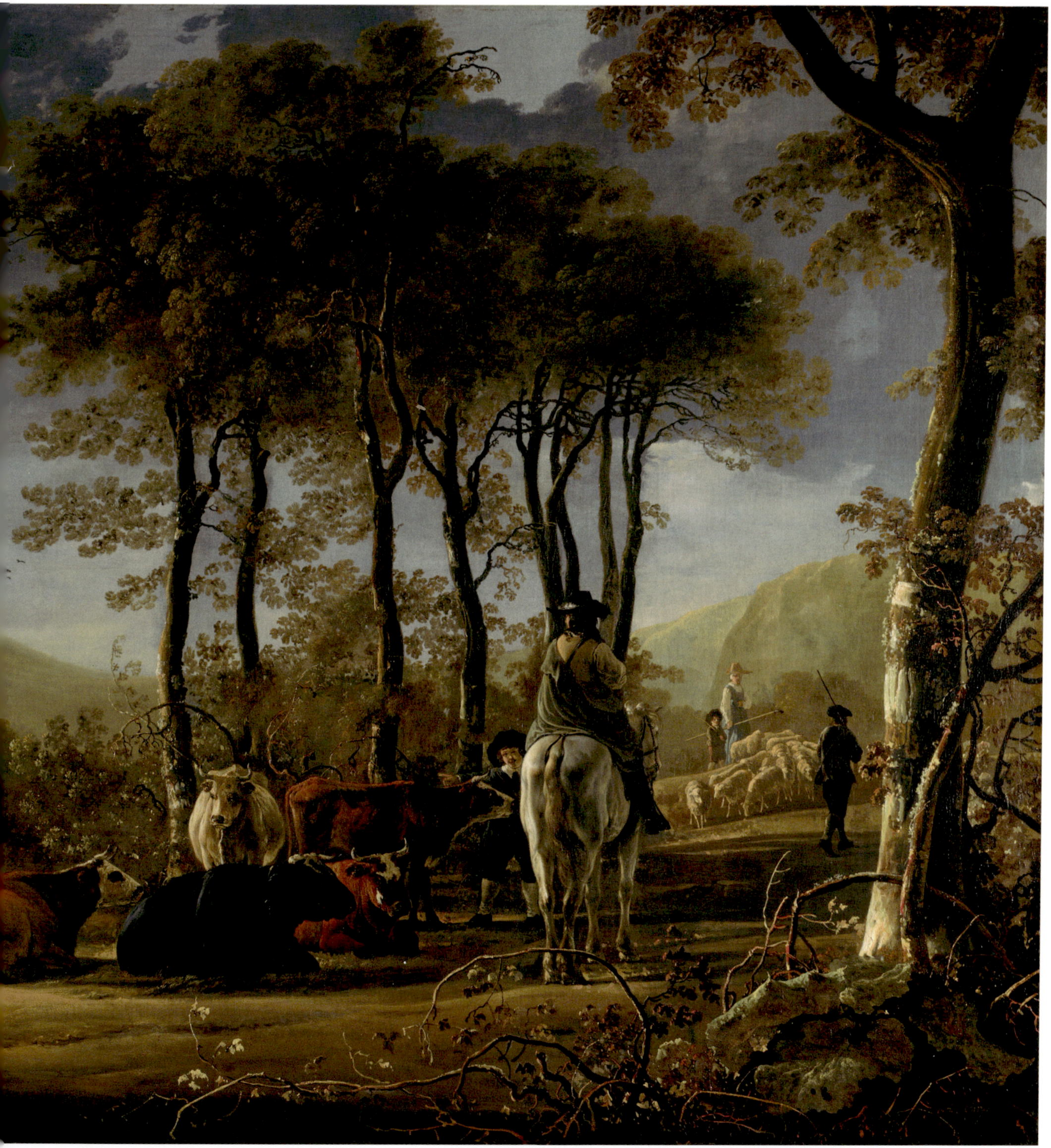

Aelbert Cuyp

(1620–1691)

River Landscape with Horseman and Peasants, about 1658–60

Oil on canvas, 123 x 241 cm
Bought with the assistance of the National Heritage Memorial Fund and The Art Fund, 1989

This magisterial landscape is one of the crowning achievements of seventeenth-century Dutch landscape painting. Along a broad path, a horseman stops to converse with a herdsman; almost unnoticed in this peaceful view is a hunter, who crouches in the bushes and takes aim at some ducks gliding through the glassy water. The view is imaginary, but the evocation of pastoral calm and warm sunlight are more important than a specific location. This spectacular light was a particular trademark of the artist, and he was in masterful command of its effects: note the delicacy of the glowing clouds and the gilt edges of the wiry foreground brambles.

River Landscape was probably painted for one of Cuyp's patrons in his native Dordrecht, but in the eighteenth and nineteenth centuries, British connoisseurs collected his paintings with equal enthusiasm. Cuyp's lyrical evocations of golden sunlight had a profound effect on later British landscape painting.

pp. 60–1

Salomon van Ruysdael

(1600/3?–1670)

A View of Deventer seen from the North-West, 1657

Oil on wood, 51.8 x 76.5 cm
Presented by William Edward Brandt, Henry Augustus Brandt, Walter Augustus Brandt and Alice Mary Bleecker in memory of Rudolph Ernst Brandt, 1962

In the sixteenth century Dutch landscape painters crafted richly detailed, brightly coloured and completely imaginary scenes that had little to do with the world around them. But beginning in the 1620s a group of Haarlem artists – including Ruysdael, Jan van Goyen, and Pieter de Molijn – began producing more realistic views of the local countryside. Their fresh consideration of the native landscape may have been inspired by nationalism, civic pride, or even by a growing desire among city-dwellers to cast aside urban cares for pastoral contentment – at least the sampling offered within a picture's frame. Restricted in palette and with a narrow focus on the simple beauty of the everyday, these modest 'tonal' landscapes completely revolutionised Dutch landscape painting.

Here Salomon van Ruysdael, uncle of Jacob van Ruisdael (pp. 80–3), shows his understanding of the luminous watery expanses that are such a feature of the Dutch topography. The low horizon and long, sweeping brushstrokes echo the flatness of the land, broken only by boats and the distant profile of the city of Deventer.

pp. 64–5

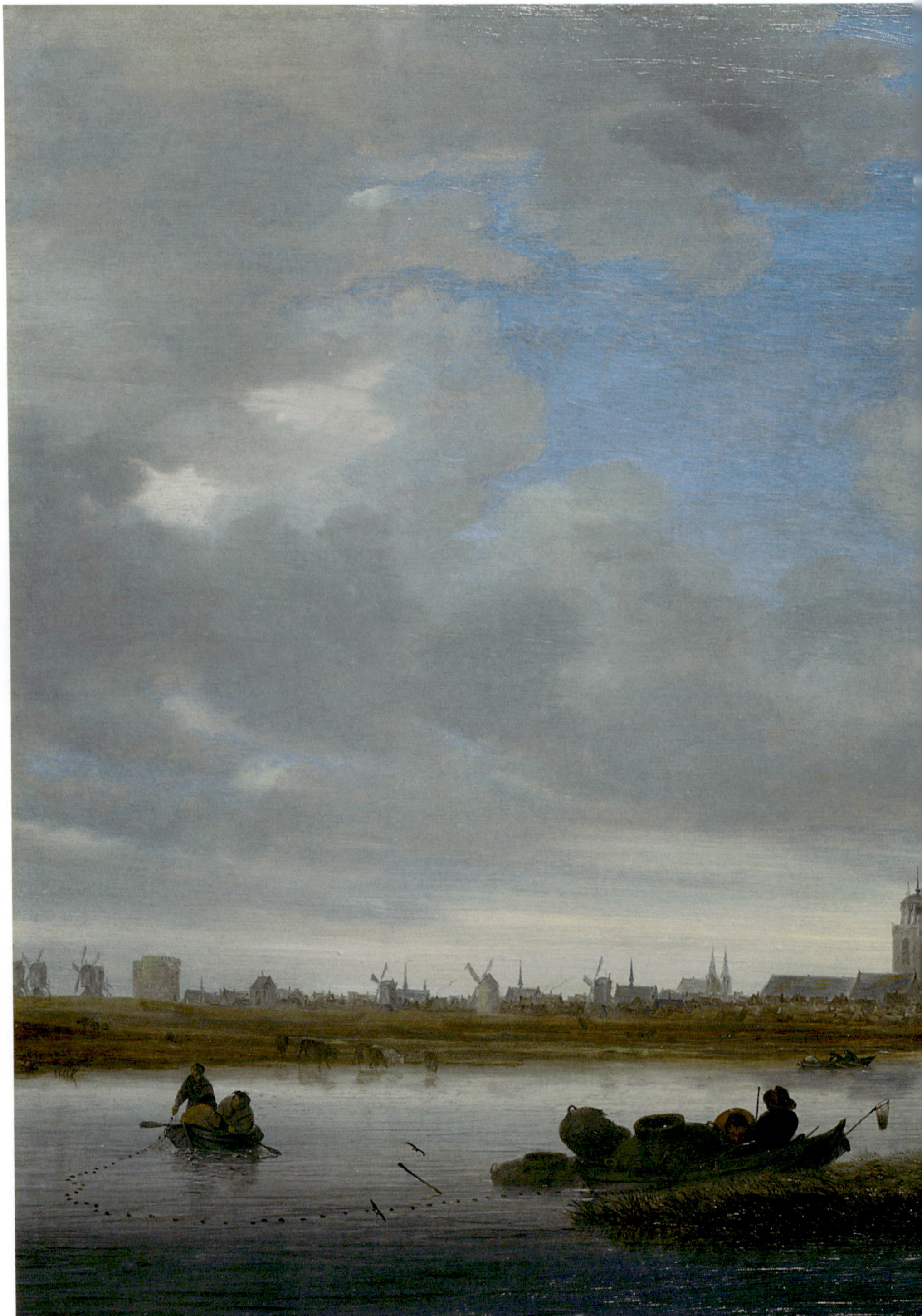

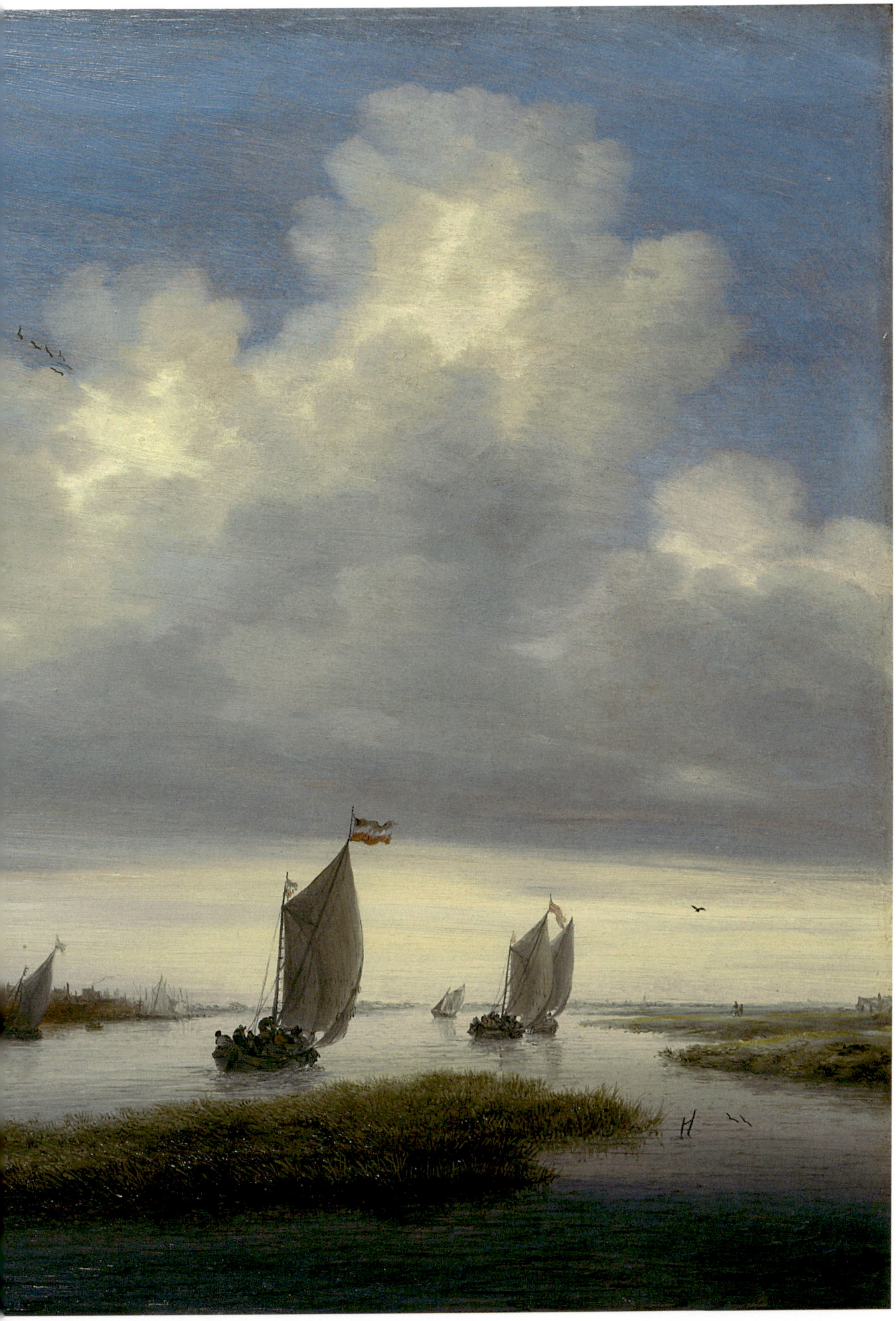

Jan Steen

(1626–1679)

Skittle Players outside an Inn, probably 1660–3

Oil on oak, 33.5 x 27 cm
Salting Bequest, 1910

Residents of Holland's crowded cities sought recreation in outings to the many inns dotted throughout the Dutch countryside. In 1651, a Frenchman living in Leiden commented on the popularity of these holiday jaunts: 'Whenever one goes [into the countryside], one finds as many people as would be seen elsewhere in a public procession. All these excursions end up at one of the inns which are ... always packed with visitors, and the confused murmur of many voices is like the sound in a city square. These are inexpensive pleasures which all, even the humblest labourer, can share.' Although the inn Steen depicted was probably not a specific landmark, he included an identifying signboard with an image of a swan. The earthenware beer jug hanging from the signpost was a broad advertisement of the inn's refreshing fare.

Steen's skillful brushwork is particularly evident in rendering the effects of light: note the sunlight edging the trunks and delicate foliage of the trees, glinting through the boards of the hoarding, and tracing the rails and posts of the rough wooden fence.

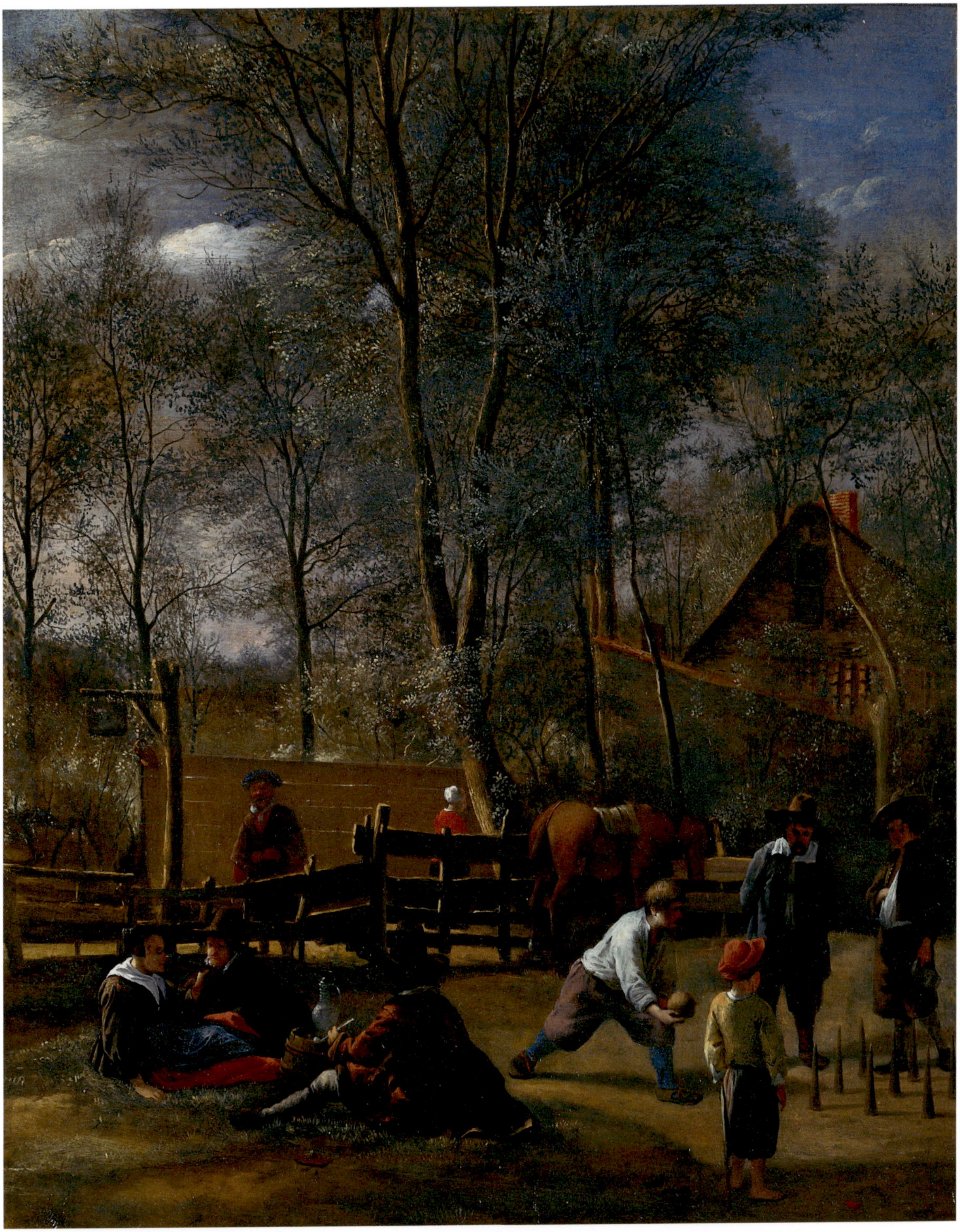

Jan Steen

(1626–1679)

The Effects of Intemperance, about 1663–5

Oil on wood, 76 x 106.5 cm

Steen is famous for boisterous paintings filled with allusions to traditional proverbs and customs: images that set the popular conception of tidy Dutch households on its head. The central figure in this drama is a housewife and mother who has fallen deeply asleep. She has drunk too much wine, or been lulled by the narcotic effects of the tobacco pipe dangling from her slack fingertips. As she slumbers, chaos reigns: her purse is picked by a small child as others gleefully feed a pie to the cat. A girl encourages the parrot – often interpreted as a mimic of human behaviour – to drink; the remaining child illustrates a Dutch proverb by tossing roses (we might say pearls) before a swine.

The basket overhead reminds us that no good will come of this free-for-all. It contains objects associated with punishment, poverty and disease, such as a birch switch, a crutch and a leper's clapper. Many of the other accessories in the scene – the silk dresses, the exotic parrot – are evidence of wealth and social standing, a reminder that even well-to-do parents must set a proper example for their children.

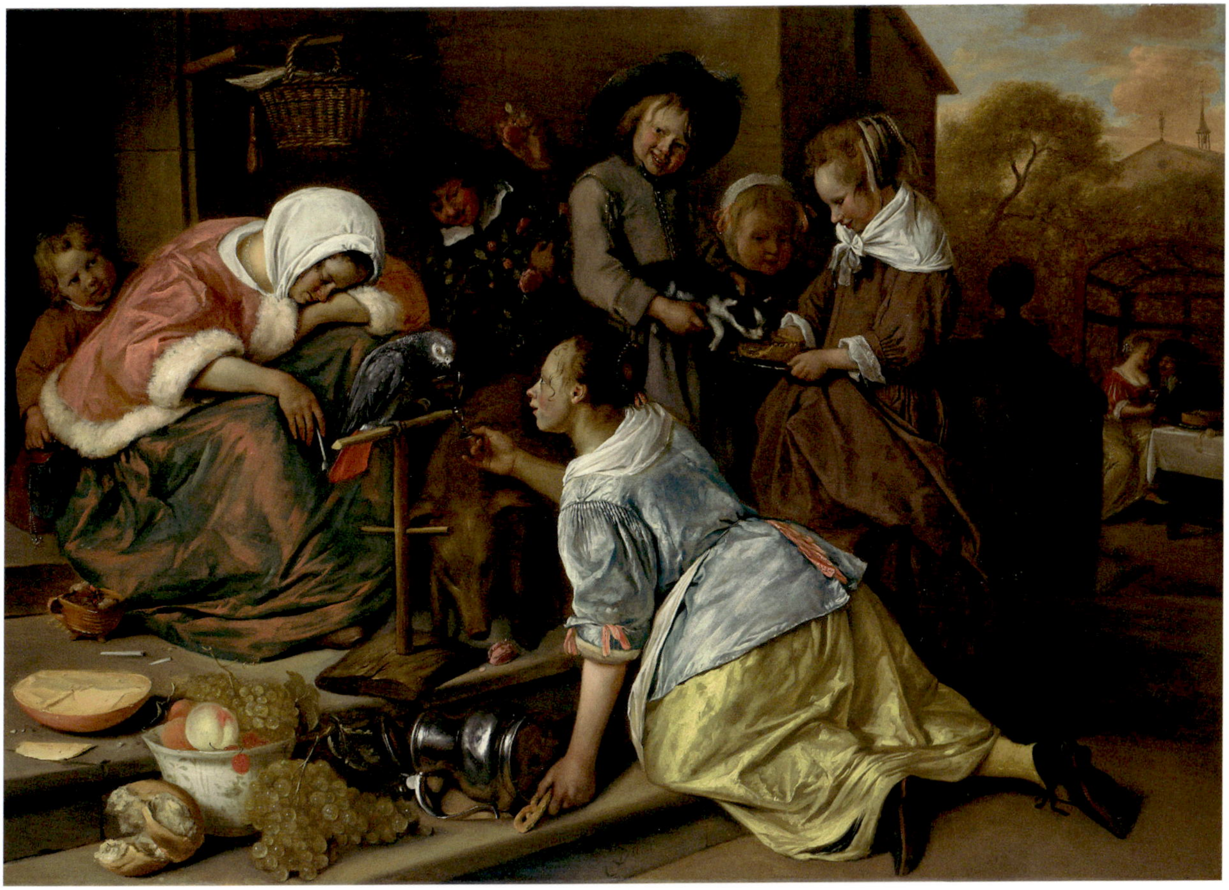

Willem van de Velde

(1633–1707)

Dutch Vessels close Inshore at Low Tide, and Men Bathing, 1661

Oil on canvas, 63.2 x 72.2 cm
Purchased with the Peel collection, 1871

The Dutch Republic of the seventeenth century was tied inextricably to the sea. Natural ports, fine ships and skilled mariners were vital factors in the nation's economic development and strategic defence, and enabled global exploration and expansion. The Dutch maritime experience spawned advances in cartography, ship design and navigation; but dependence on the sea came at a price – its fierce power was an omnipresent threat as storms and floods regularly threatened the low-lying nation.

Willem van de Velde, the greatest seventeenth-century Dutch marine painter, studied with his father, Willem van de Velde the Elder, and worked with him for much of his career. After 1672, the two painters moved to England and established a studio at the Queen's House, Greenwich. This scene is typical of the serene and subtly atmospheric views of ships in calm waters that Van de Velde the younger perfected during the 1660s. Towering skies are reflected in smooth water, creating a silent world that seems to glow with limpid light.

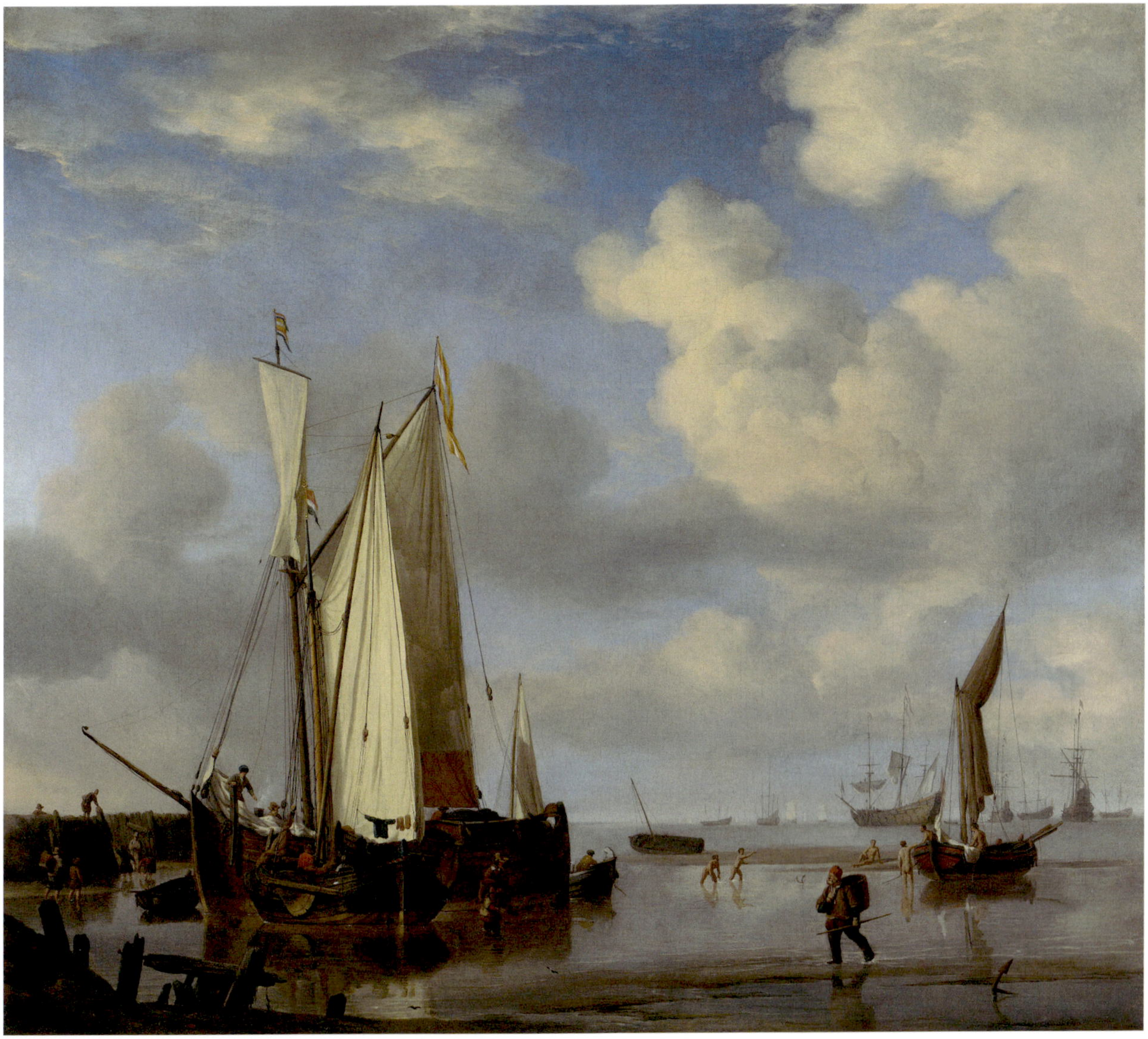

Jan van der Heyden

(1637–1712)

View of the Westerkerk, Amsterdam, probably 1660

Oil on oak, 90.7 x 114.5 cm

Van der Heyden pioneered the development of Dutch cityscape painting, recording canals, churches, castles and courtyards with imaginative flair and remarkable detail. The centrepiece here is Amsterdam's Westerkerk, designed in 1620 by Hendrick de Keyser, father of the painter Thomas de Keyser (p. 32). It was the largest Protestant church built up to that time, with classicising details that reflected the latest cosmopolitan taste. Van der Heyden's consummate concern for detail is evident at every turn: individually delineated bricks and paving stones, a dog relieving itself, and tattered flyers advertising a sale of paintings.

The unusually large size of *View of the Westerkerk* was undoubtedly dictated by the church's governors, who commissioned the painting. Although Van der Heyden frequently manipulated elements within a scene in favour of overall effect, his view of the Westerkerk is immediately recognisable – even so, he teases our curiosity by obscuring portions of the building behind a screen of trees.

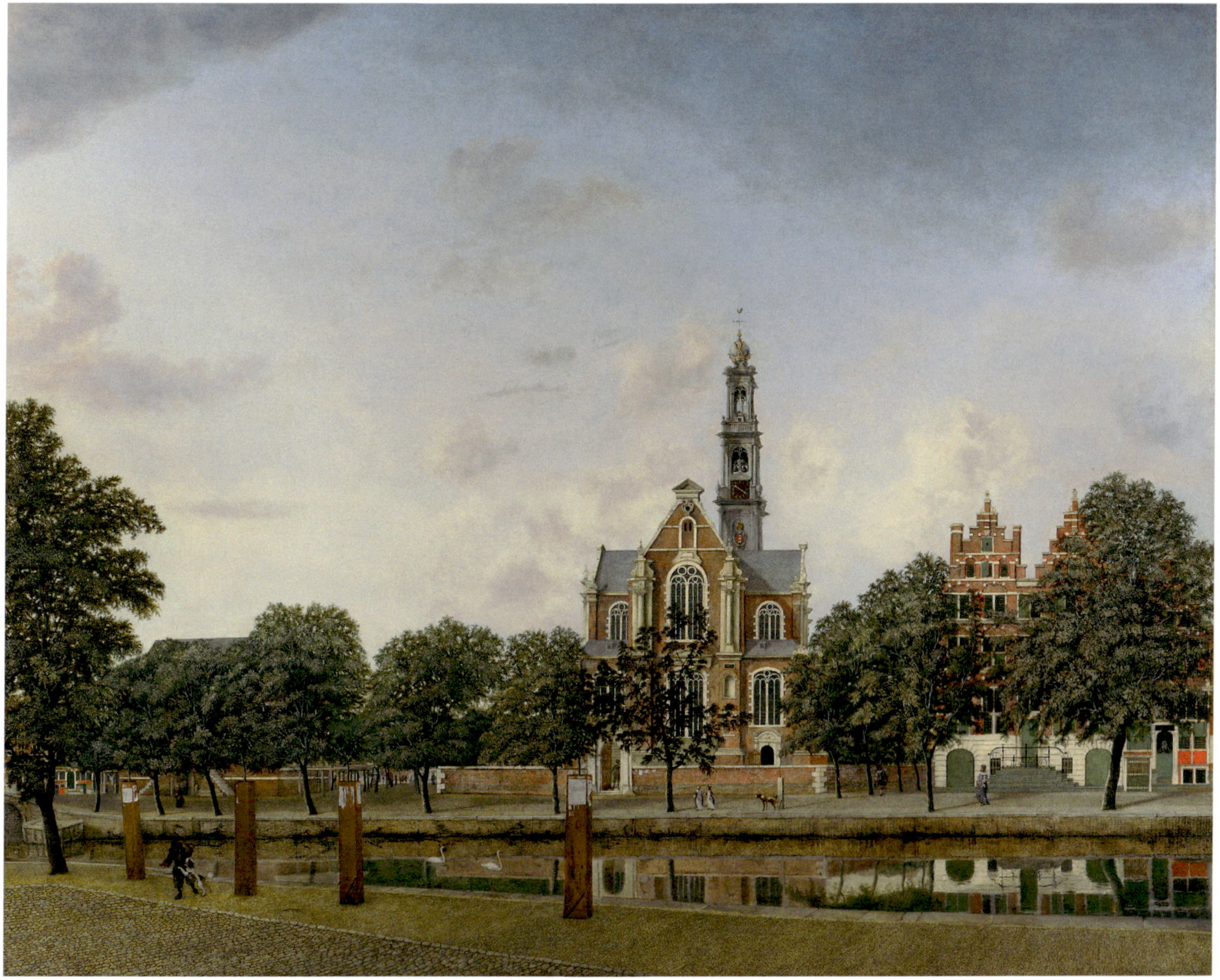

Emanuel de Witte

(1615/17–1691/2)

The Interior of the Oude Kerk, Amsterdam, during a Sermon, about 1660

Oil on canvas, 79.1 x 63.1 cm
Presented by the Misses Rachel F. and Jean I. Alexander; entered the Collection in 1972

A group of women and children, some studying their Bibles, listen attentively to the energetic preacher as the city's burghers, screened off from the foreground group, crowd into the south aisle of Amsterdam's Oude Kerk. Light streaming through tall windows accentuates crisp white collars and casts dark shadows on the stone floor. De Witte, who began his career as a figure painter, highlights the propriety of the Dutch people through the proper behaviour of this foreground group: these devout citizens are a testament to the importance of the sermon in the liturgy of the Dutch Reformed Church.

Unlike Saenredam's conspicuously spare church interiors (p. 29), De Witte's image is busy and more richly decorated. These embellishments draw the eye into the depths of the church, and on to the roofscape seen through the right-hand window (which features Amsterdam's coat of arms on the central roundel), into the city beyond.

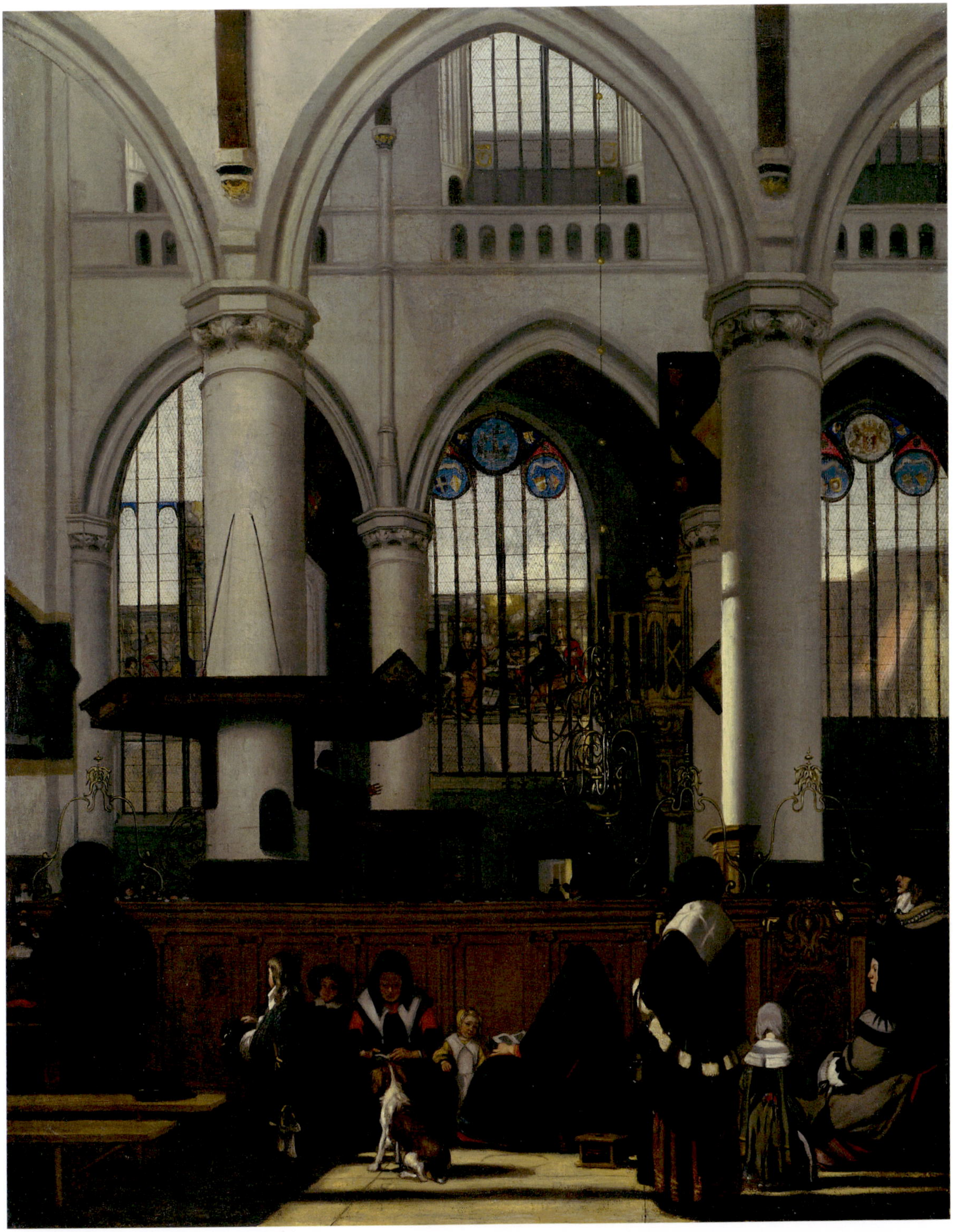

Adriaen van Ostade

(1610–1685)

An Alchemist, 1661

Oil on oak, 34 x 45.2 cm
Purchased with the Peel collection, 1871

In the seventeenth century, alchemy, the attempt to isolate 'pure' matter (most commonly extracting gold from base metals), developed into a separate discipline that provided important prerequisites for chemistry and medicine. Despite many scholarly publications, however, most people viewed it as a vain and mystical pseudo-science – although images (often humorous or satirical) of ardent experimenters were popular from early in the sixteenth century. Its practice was equated to a blind pursuit of wealth, and viewed as a paradigm of human folly.

Ostade's depiction of a shabby practitioner intent on his experiments is at once sympathetic and caricatured. The cavernous interior is filled with the chaotic detritus of the alchemist's humble existence. Beneath the wooden stool is a paper bearing the Latin inscription 'oleum et operam perdis' (to lose one's time and trouble). Spectacles allude to the alchemist's inability to perceive the futility of his experiments; the empty moneybag on the ground nearby suggests the resources lost in the pursuit of greater wealth.

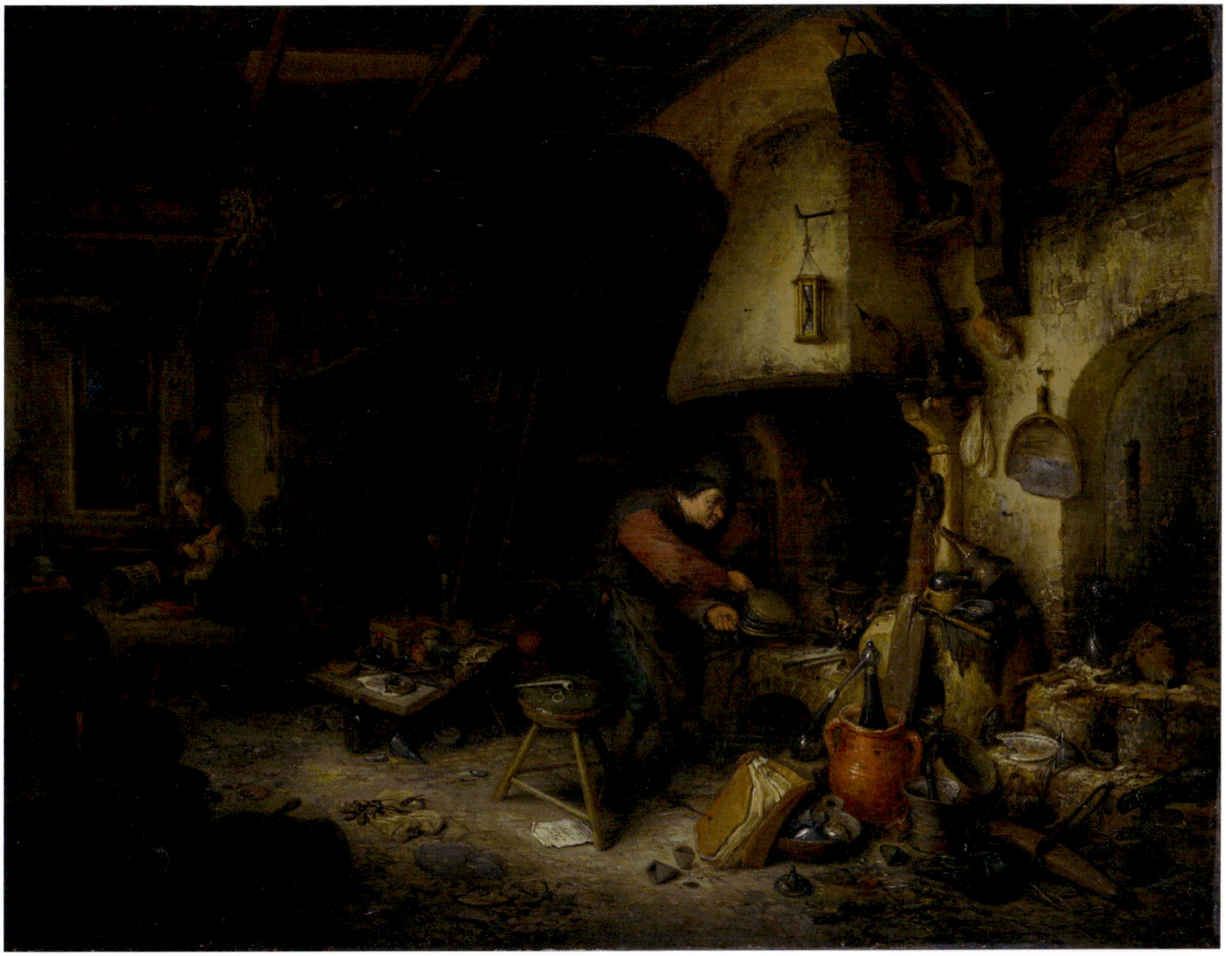

Gerrit Dou

(1613–1675)

A Poulterer's Shop, about 1670

Oil on oak, 58 x 46 cm
Purchased with the Peel collection, 1871

In 1628, the young Gerrit Dou became Rembrandt's first pupil in Leiden. Although initially the two artists' styles were quite close, their paths soon diverged: Rembrandt progressed towards a broader, freer manner of painting while Dou pursued a precise and highly finished technique capable of dazzling illusionistic effects. His gem-like paintings attracted wealthy patrons and inspired a school of younger artists, known collectively as the Leiden *fijnschilders* ('fine painters').

The *Poulterer's Shop* is a brilliant example of Dou's playful approach to space and his astonishing ability to differentiate tactile surfaces. The wares on the poulterer's counter are a *tour de force* of texture: sleek plumage and cold, pimpled flesh; the metallic sheen of the market pail and the soft fur of the hare. Many of Dou's paintings contain symbolic visual references that hint at other 'readings'. The Dutch word *vogel* (bird) was often synonymous with the phallus, *voglen* (to bird) was a euphemism for sexual intercourse, and the hare was associated with lust.

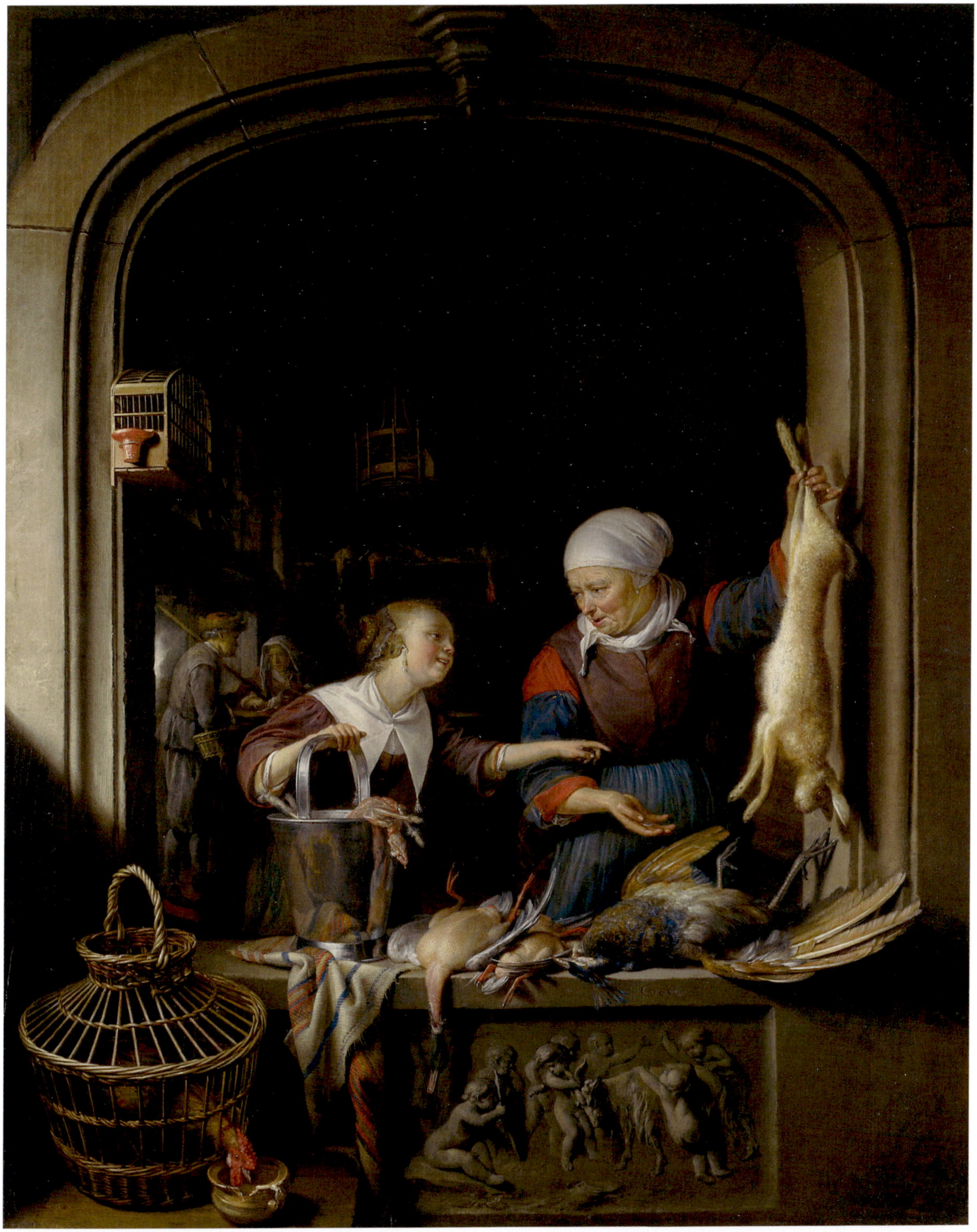

Jacob van Ruisdael

(1628/9?–1682)

A Landscape with a Ruined Castle and a Church, about 1665–70

Oil on canvas, 109 x 146 cm
Wynn Ellis Bequest, 1876

One of the most distinctive developments in Dutch landscape painting of the Golden Age was the wide panoramic view of Holland's ubiquitous flat plains. This was not the encyclopaedic 'world landscape' favoured by sixteenth-century Flemish artists, but a more naturalistic view characterised by a lowered vantage point and a delight in everyday motifs. Often a relatively low horizon emphasised the expansive vistas afforded by flat terrain beneath an enormous open sky.

Jacob van Ruisdael was one of the most gifted practitioners of the Dutch panoramic landscape. This scene has been described as depicting fields surrounding Haarlem or Beverwijk, or in Gooiland, a district east of Amsterdam, but in fact the heroic landscape is a product entirely of the artist's imagination, a plausible assemblage of motifs observed from nature. The work exemplifies Ruisdael's masterful balance of light and shadow, of precise detail and boundless space. Dark clouds power across a vast sky, permitting isolated patches of pale lemony light to fall upon open fields, shocks of harvested grain, and the sails of a windmill. In the foreground, a glassy pond mirrors the grey sky and the ruins of the castle at right.

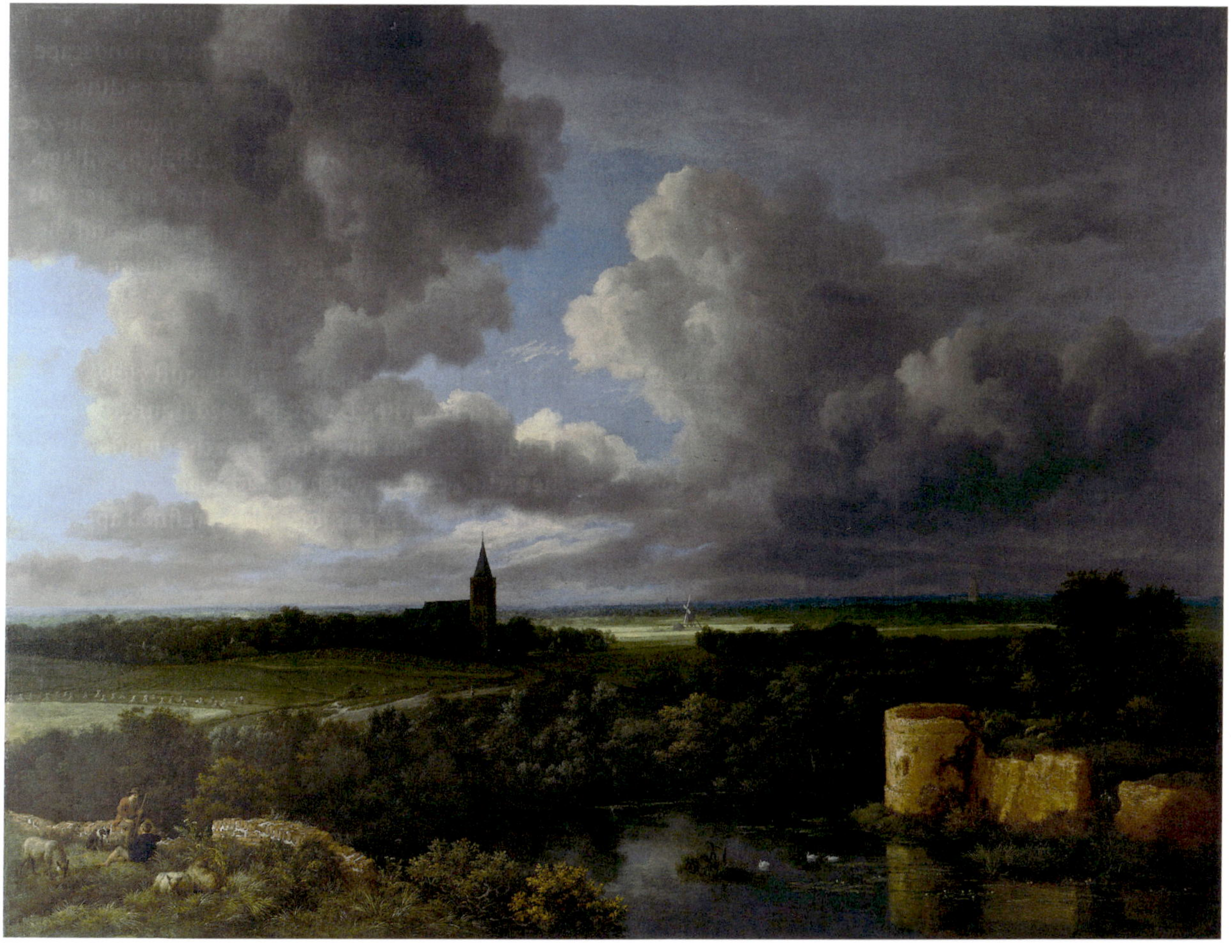

Jacob van Ruisdael

(1628/9?–1682)

The Shore at Egmond-aan-Zee, about 1675

Oil on canvas, 53.7 x 66.2 cm

Unlike many painters who restricted themselves to a narrow area of specialisation, Ruisdael turned his hand to an astonishing array of landscape subjects. This view is one of the artist's rare images of the sandy coastline bordering the North Sea. Situated north-west of Amsterdam, Egmond-aan-Zee was settled in about 977 and over the centuries prospered as a fishing village. Egmond's relationship to the sea was an uneasy one, however, as the area was (and is) subject to dramatic coastal erosion: in 1741 thirty-six houses and the church of St Agnes – its tower is visible at the right of the composition – were subsumed by the waves.

The sea's harsh power is tamed in Ruisdael's elegant and tranquil view, though dark, windswept clouds loom overhead. Well-dressed figures promenade, enjoying the pale sunshine that filters through the clouds. The painting dates from late in the artist's career, when he had abandoned the dramatic intensity of his earlier landscapes for a more subtle, refined approach.

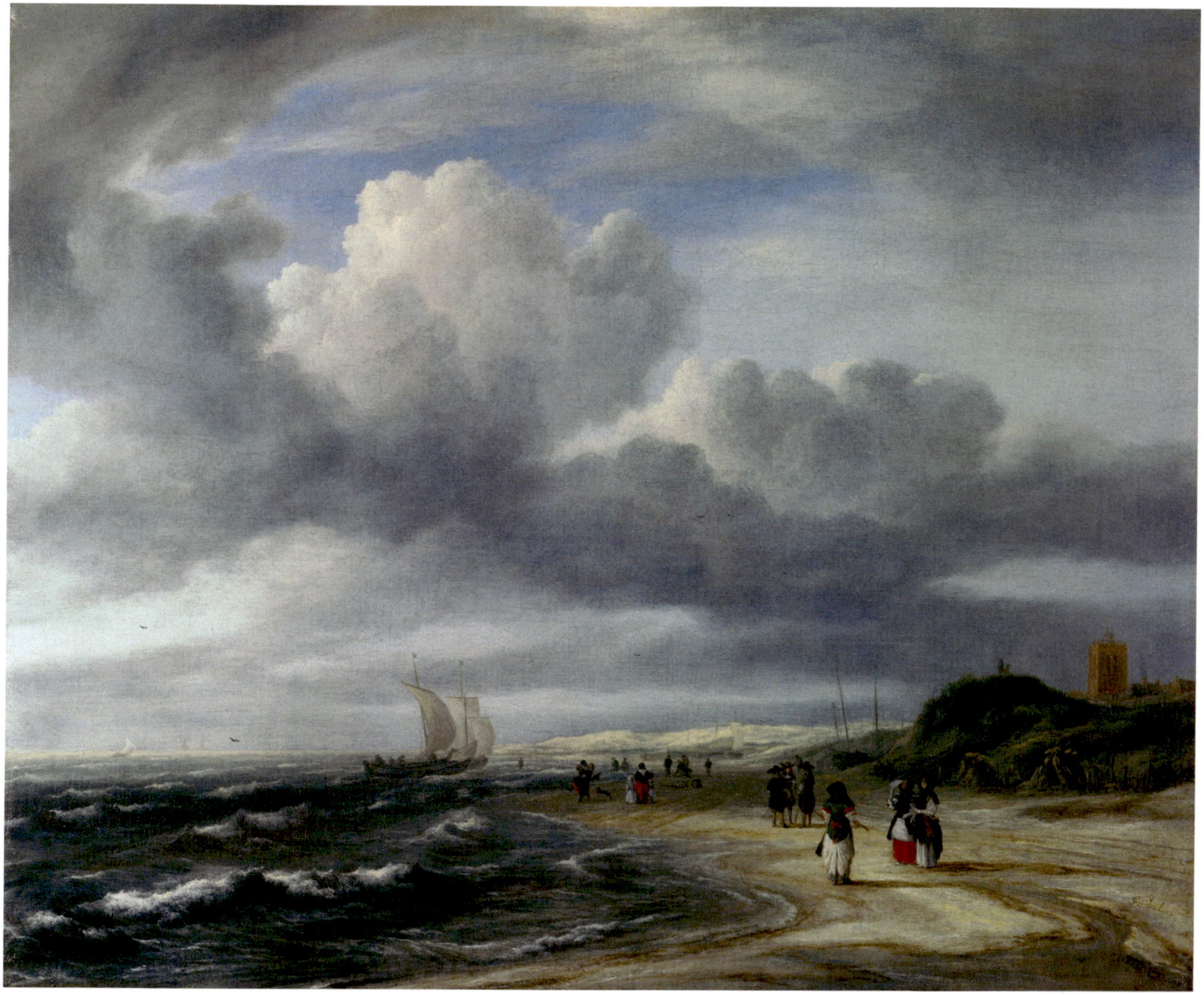

Johannes Vermeer

(1632–1675)

A Young Woman standing at a Virginal, about 1670–2

Oil on canvas, 51.7 x 45.2 cm

Vermeer is best known for his preternaturally serene depictions of domestic interiors, featuring just one or two figures engaged in mundane pursuits. Although his compositions appear quite simple, each element is precisely placed to achieve a perfect balance of light, colour, form and texture within the scene. Individual motifs are recorded with the barest essentials; Vermeer's unique sensitivity to the way light illuminates objects imparts a delicate luminosity to his works. Today Vermeer's paintings are world famous, but in his own day he was scarcely known outside of Delft, and most of his meagre output – less than three dozen paintings are known today – was acquired by one local collector.

A young woman, stylishly clad in a white satin gown, stands at the precise centre of this painting. The room is elegant but spare; the few furnishings – a chair, a virginal, and two paintings – indicate a prosperous home. Brilliant sunlight creates crisp accents on the folds of the woman's dress, the gold picture frame and the edges of the virginal case. Just behind the woman's head is a painting of a Cupid holding a card aloft. The image is taken from a popular emblem advocating faithfulness and the love of one over the love of many. Vermeer's painting has been interpreted as an image of pure, harmonious love – a message sensed in the clarity and harmony of the composition itself.

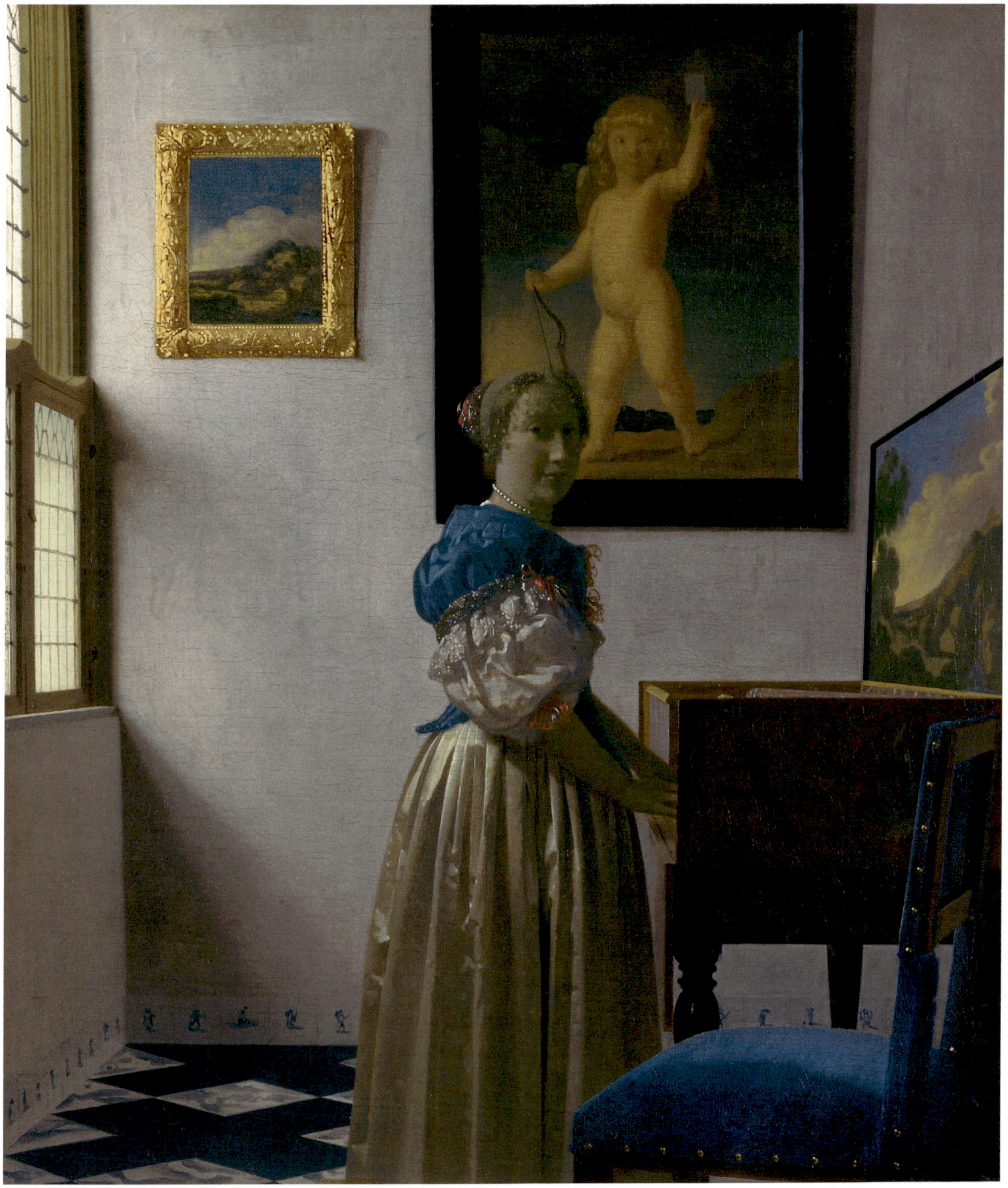

Johannes Vermeer

(1632–1675)

A Young Woman seated at a Virginal, about 1670–2

Oil on canvas, 51.5 x 45.5 cm
Salting Bequest, 1910

The Gallery's two paintings by Vermeer have often been considered as pendants, but they certainly represent variations on a theme that had occupied Vermeer throughout much of his career: the relationship between love and music. Both were executed late in the artist's career, when his painting technique had become extraordinarily simplified, almost abstract. In this painting, for example, details such as the trim on the woman's sleeve, or the edge of the chair back, are suggested with expressive dribbles and clots of paint.

Young Woman seated at a Virginal presents a more complex view of the interplay between love and music than *Young Woman standing at a Virginal* (p. 85). Instead of clear daylight, the room seems dimly lit by flickering candlelight; instead of pure, insistent geometry, we encounter oblique angles and softly crumpled fabrics. Perhaps the most striking contrast is the painting hanging on the back wall: in this instance a work by the Utrecht painter Dirck van Baburen, showing a scene of prostitution. While this might suggest that Vermeer intended an allusion to illicit love, the viola da gamba in the foreground could indicate a more chaste reading. One stringed instrument was said to resonate when another was played, just as two loving hearts existed in harmony.

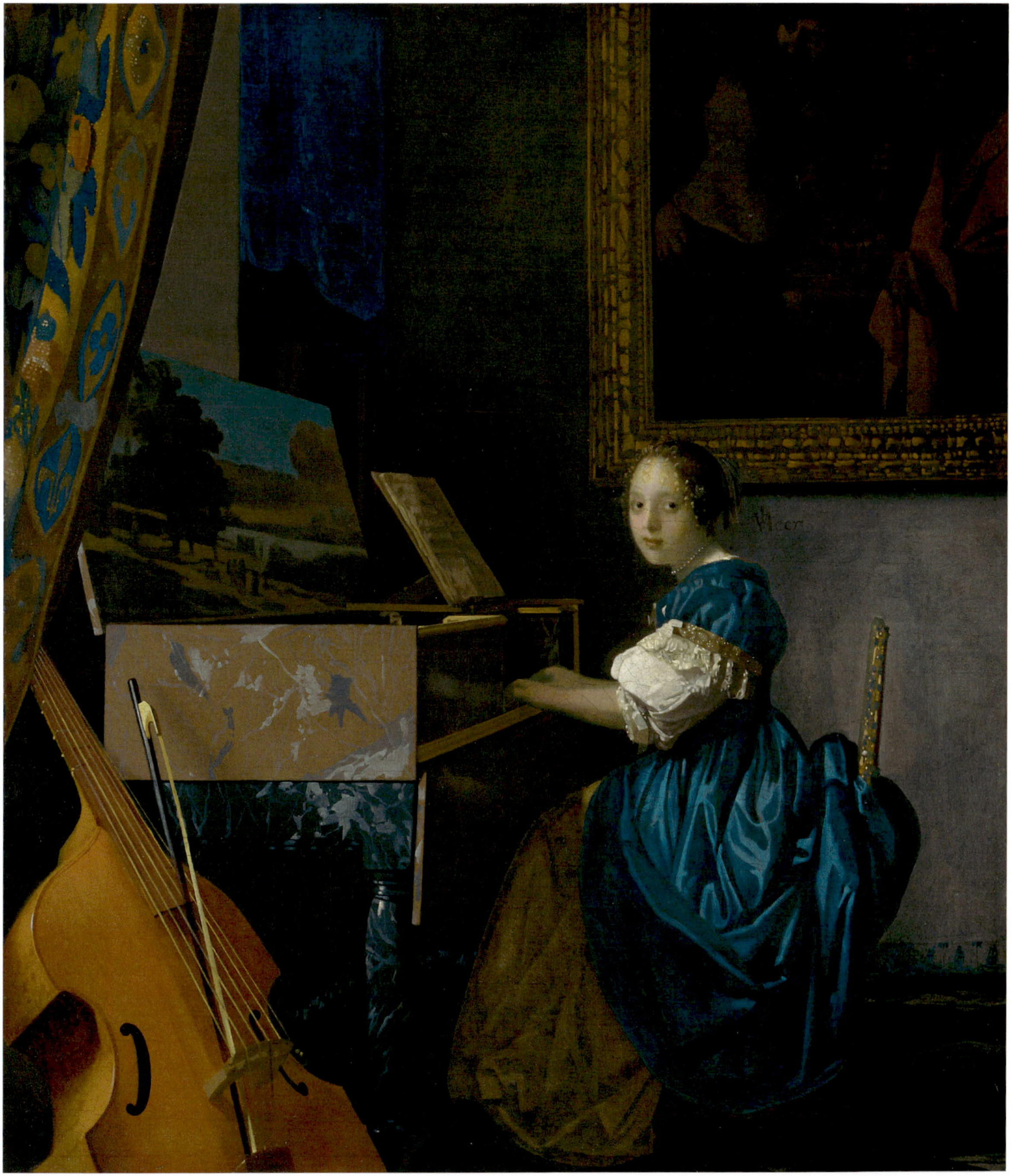

Meindert Hobbema

(1638–1709)

The Haarlem Lock, Amsterdam, about 1663–5

Oil on canvas, 77 x 98 cm
Bequeathed by Miss Beatrice Mildmay, 1953

Hobbema was a pupil of Jacob van Ruisdael (pp. 80–3) in Amsterdam in the late 1650s, but soon developed his own distinctive style. His scenes of the Dutch countryside are characterised by a deft interplay of sunlight and cool shadow, with verdant masses of shrubbery punctuated by luminous views glimpsed through a screen of trees (p. 91). This is the artist's only known cityscape.

Dominating the foreground is the Haarlem Lock (or Haarlemmersluis), which connected the Singel canal within the city walls to the river IJ outside. To the right is the Herring-Packers' Tower, originally part of the city's fifteenth-century fortifications, with a lacy 'modern' tower added on top in the seventeenth century. The lock bustles with activity: the keeper opens the gate, releasing a rush of water into the canal. Within the lock we see the heads of two boatmen as their boat descends; in the canal at right another boatman struggles to hold his small vessel against the flow. Haarlem Lock was undoubtedly a familiar sight to Hobbema, since by 1668 (and probably earlier) he was living just around the corner.

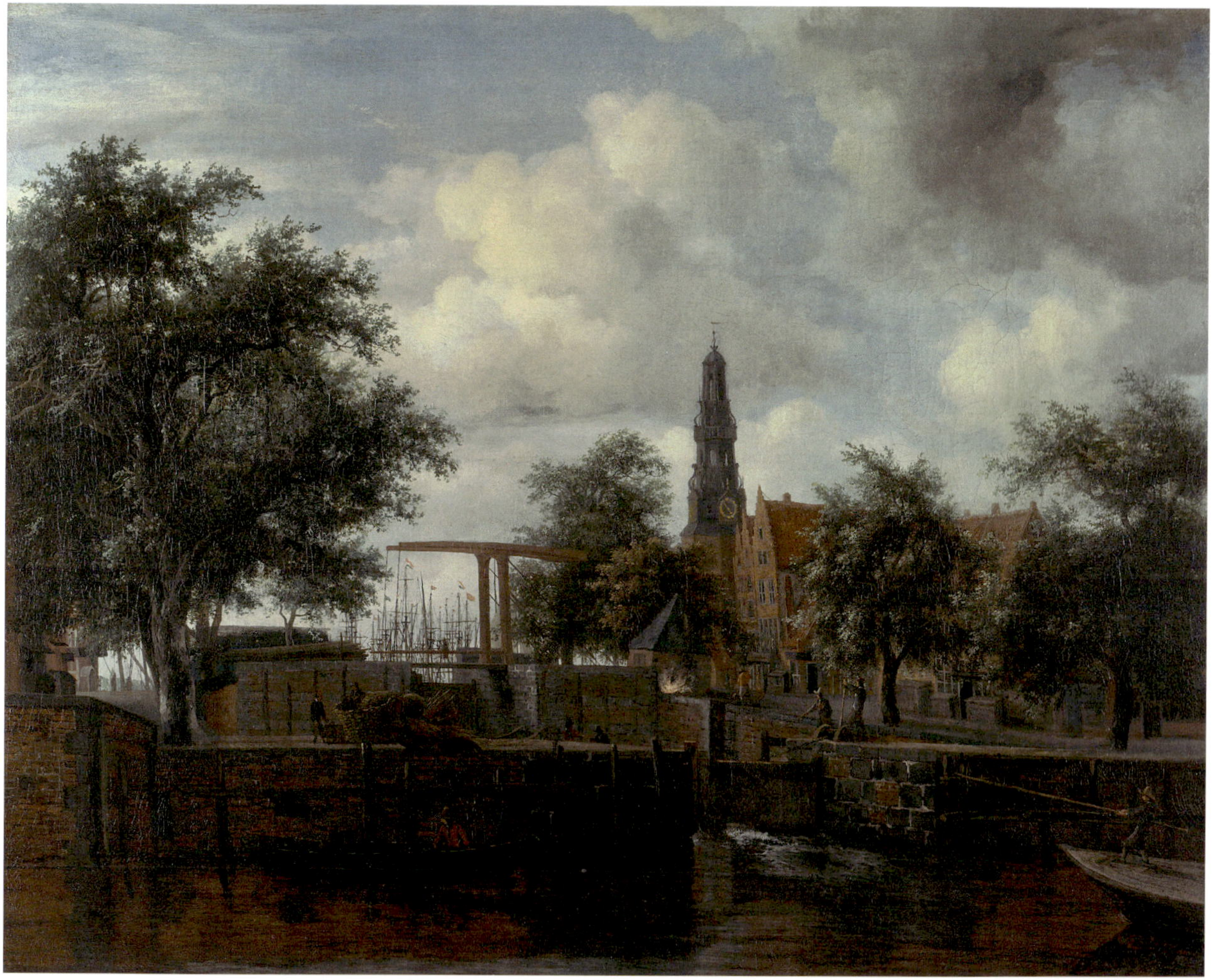

Meindert Hobbema

(1638–1709)

The Avenue at Middelharnis, 1689

Oil on canvas, 103.5 x 141 cm
Purchased with the Peel collection, 1871

In this remarkably tranquil painting, Hobbema focuses on documenting the well-ordered landscape on the outskirts of the town of Middelharnis in southern Holland. Slender trees, pruned of their lateral branches, form a natural colonnade either side of a dirt road, but X-radiographs reveal that Hobbema painted out the two trees closest to the picture plane, thereby widening the foreground to exaggerate the recession of the path. The spacious foreground and low horizon invite the viewer to stroll towards the town, crossing paths with the hunter and his dog. The elaborate spire of the fifteenth-century church of St Michael signals the destination. Carefully tended by a gardener, the tidy plant nurseries on the right epitomise nature tamed.

The classical serenity of Hobbema's composition contrasts with his earlier works, which are characterised by masses of abundant foliage, rather than a single dominant feature. This landscape was made over twenty years after Hobbema had ostensibly abandoned painting to become a wine-gauger for the city of Amsterdam.

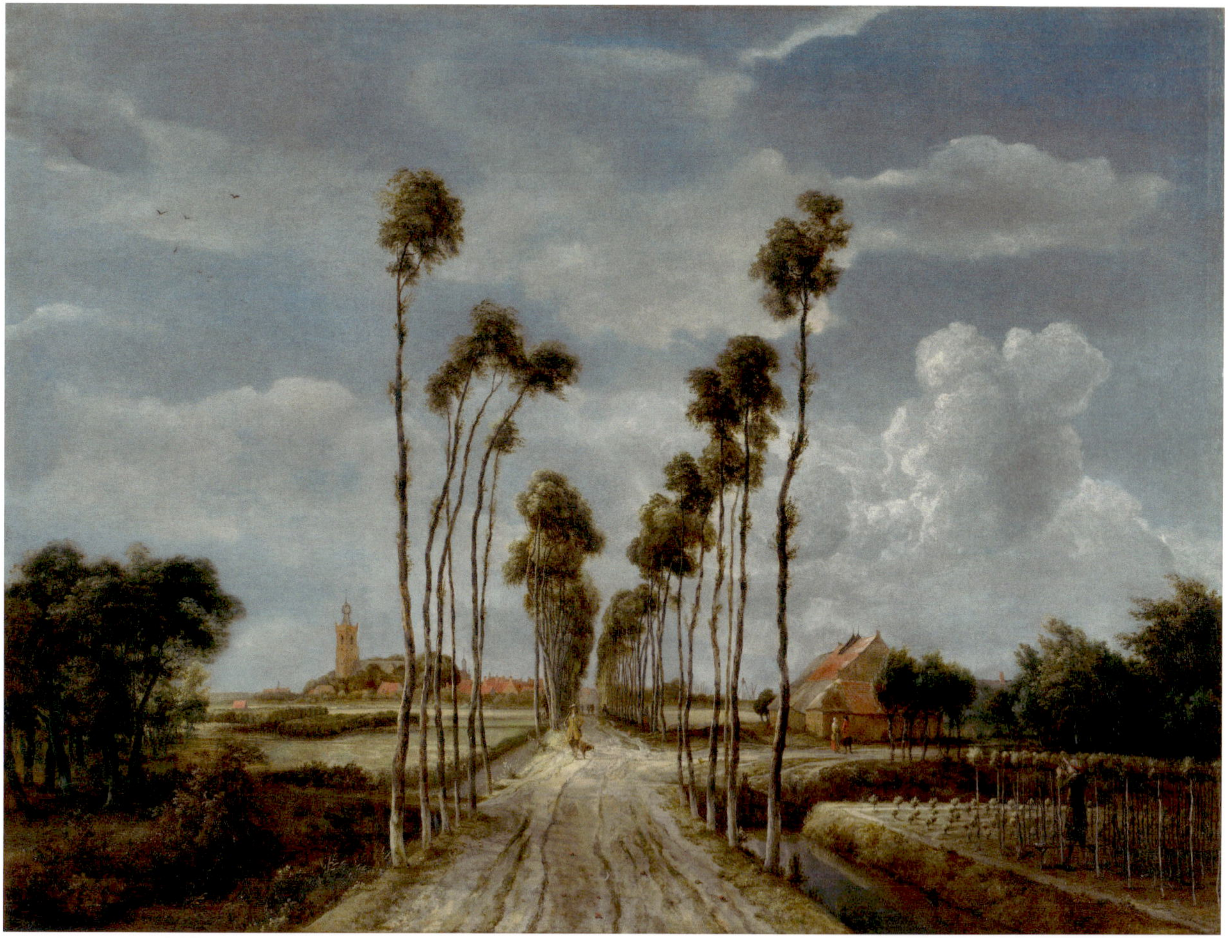

Gerrit Berckheyde

(1638–1698)

The Market Place and the Grote Kerk at Haarlem, 1674

Oil on canvas, 51.8 x 67 cm

In the seventeenth century, the impressive market place (Grote Markt) of Haarlem was the hub of the city's commercial, political and religious life, dominated by the boxy mass of the Grote Kerk. Dedicated to Saint Bavo, patron saint of Haarlem, the church was begun in the fourteenth century, with the spire added in 1520. The low stalls to the north of the church, which housed the city's fish market, have since been removed. The building with the tall stepped gable immediately to the right of the church is the meat market (Vleeshal), one of the most important Renaissance buildings in the Netherlands, designed by Lieven de Key and constructed in 1602/3.

Unlike Van der Heyden (p. 73), Berckheyde favoured views of open squares bounded by monuments. He painted numerous views of the market place in his native city of Haarlem, from different angles and at different times of day. This stately painting shows the square lit by rays of late-afternoon sun. The light casts dramatic shadows across the foreground of the scene, and sets the silhouetted Vleeshal against the brilliantly lit façade of the Grote Kerk.

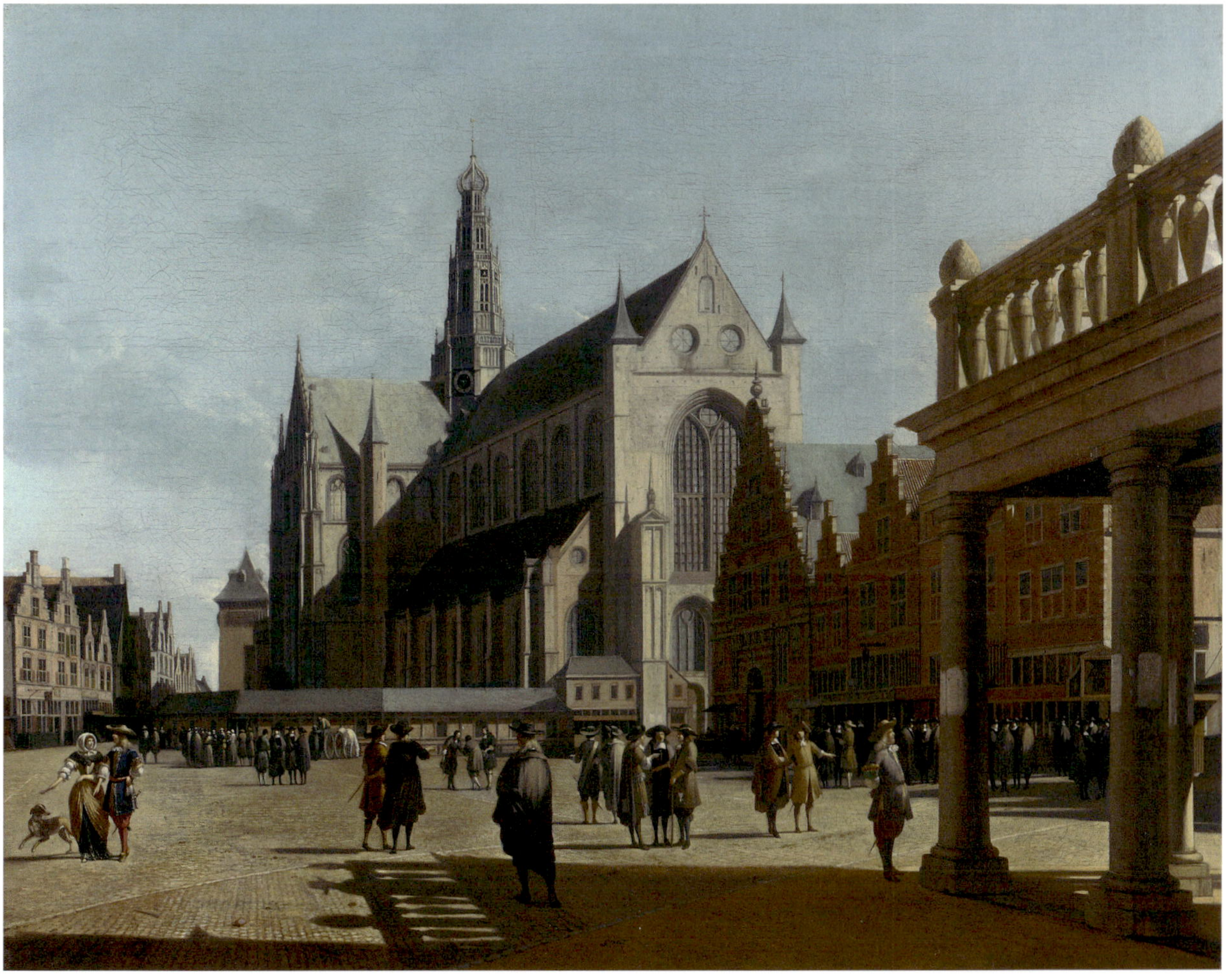

Jan van Huysum

(1682–1749)

Flowers in a Terracotta Vase, 1736–7

Oil on canvas, 133.5 x 91.5 cm

Exotic flowers were a luxurious status symbol in the seventeenth and eighteenth centuries, and extraordinary prices were paid for the rarest examples. Consequently, although the general popularity of still-life painting declined during the period, meticulously rendered flower paintings remained fashionable. Van Huysum cast aside the dark backgrounds and stark lighting favoured by earlier seventeenth-century artists (p. 19) for luminous compositions brimming with colour and variety. An early biographer noted that when the artist began to lighten his backgrounds, the value of his paintings soared. Paintings such as this, with arrangements set within illusionistic stone niches, were often commissioned as over-mantels for the fashionable dining rooms of wealthy patrons.

Van Huysum draws attention to a costly blue hyacinth by placing it against gold and white narcissi, and balances highly prized white tulips 'flamed' with red against vibrant poppies. The array displays Van Huysum's interest in creating a harmonious overall design rather than conveying depth. For example, the eye-catching yellow narcissi seem to glow from within the bouquet, disrupting the three-dimensional illusion.

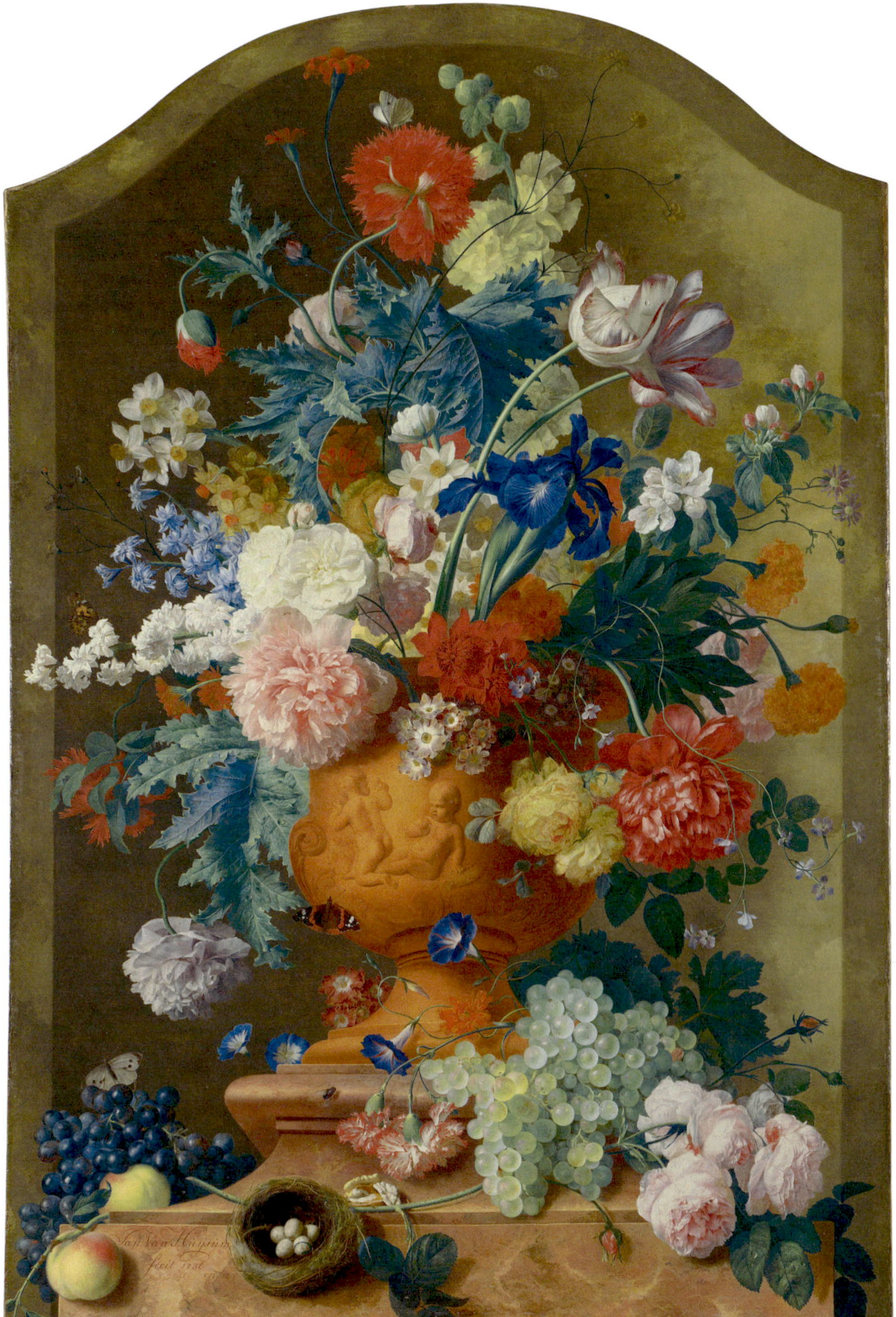
Jan Van Huysum
fecit 1736

Dutch Painting is generously supported by Horizon Asset Limited

HORIZON

All text is written by Marjorie E. Wieseman, apart from the texts on pp. 16, 28, 36, 40, 48, 58, 74, 90 and 94, which are written by Elena J. Greer.

First published in Great Britain in 2014 by
National Gallery Company Limited
St Vincent House
30 Orange Street
London WC2H 7HH

www.nationalgallery.co.uk

ISBN: 978 1 85709 579 1
1038052

British Library Cataloguing-in-Publication Data.
A catalogue record is available from the British Library.
Library of Congress Control Number: 2014934006

Publisher: Jan Green
Project Editor: Rachel Giles
Picture Researcher: Suzanne Bosman
Production: Jane Hyne and Penny Le Tissier

Designed by Joe Ewart for Society
Printed in Hong Kong by Printing Express
Origination by DL Imaging, London

Front cover: Pieter de Hooch, *A Courtyard of a House in Delft*, 1658 (detail; p. 49)

p. 2: Rembrandt, *A Woman bathing in a Stream (Hendrickje Stoffels?)*, 1654 (detail; p. 53)

pp. 4–5: Willem van de Velde, *Dutch Vessels close Inshore at Low Tide, and Men Bathing*, 1661 (detail; p. 71)

p. 6: Jan van Huysum, *Flowers in a Terracotta Vase*, 1736–7, (detail; p. 95)

pp. 14–15: Gerrit Dou, *A Poulterer's Shop*, about 1670 (detail; p. 79)

All measurements give height before width

Photographic credits:

p. 8
Left: © The National Gallery, London
Right: © White Images/Scala, Florence

p. 9
Left: © Photo Scala, Florence/BPK, Bildagentur für Kunst, Kultur und Geschichte, Berlin, photo Hans-Peter Klut
Right: © Rijksmuseum, Amsterdam

FSC
www.fsc.org
MIX
Paper from responsible sources
FSC™ C012285